YOU CAN
YOU WILL

8 UNDENIABLE QUALITIES OF A WINNER

JOEL OSTEEN

New York   Boston   Nashville

Copyright © 2014 Joel Osteen

Unless indicated, scripture quotations are taken from the Holy Bible, New Living Translation, copyright © 1996, 2004, 2007, 2013 by Tyndale House Foundation. Used by permission of Tyndale House Publishers, Inc., Carol Stream, Illinois 60188. All rights reserved.

FaithWords
Hachette Book Group
237 Park Avenue
New York, NY 10017

www.faithwords.com

Printed in the United States of America

RRD-H

First Edition: September 2014
10 9 8 7 6 5 4 3 2 1

FaithWords is a division of Hachette Book Group, Inc.
The FaithWords name and logo are trademarks of
Hachette Book Group, Inc.

The Hachette Speakers Bureau provides a wide range of authors for speaking events. To find out more, go to www.hachettespeakersbureau.com or call (866) 376-6591.

The publisher is not responsible for websites (or their content) that are not owned by the publisher.

Library of Congress Cataloging-in-Publication Data

Library of Congress data has been applied for.

ISBN 978-1-4555-7571-8 (Hardcover ed.); ISBN 978-1-4555-3015-1 (Large print ed.); ISBN 978-1-4555-5967-1 (International ed.); ISBN 978-1-4555-7840-5 (Spanish ed.); ISBN 978-1-4555-6142-1 (Autographed ed.)

*This book is dedicated to an amazing woman,
Dodie Osteen, who is now celebrating her eighty-
first year. Her love, kindness, generosity, and
strength of faith have inspired not only me but also
countless others around the world. I love her dearly
and I feel honored to call her my Mother.*

ACKNOWLEDGMENTS

Once again, I am grateful for a wonderful team of professionals who help me put this book together for you. Leading them is my publisher, Rolf Zettersten, at FaithWords/ Hachette, and Hachette Chairman and CEO Michael Pietsch, along with Patsy Jones and Laura Wheeler.

I am grateful also to my literary agents Shannon Marven and Jan Miller Rich at Dupree Miller & Associates, and especially Wes Smith, the wordsmith who helps keep my message clear.

In this book I offer many stories shared with me by friends, members of our congregation, and people I've met around the world. I appreciate and acknowledge their contributions and support. Some of those mentioned in the book are people I have not met personally, and, in a few cases, we've changed the names to protect the privacy of individuals. I give honor to all of those to whom honor is due. As the son of a church leader and a pastor myself, I've listened to countless sermons and presentations, so in some cases I can't remember the exact source of a story. Thanks to all who have touched my life with their own. My intention in writing this book is to pass on the blessings, and to God be the glory.

I am indebted to the amazing staff of Lakewood Church, the wonderful members of Lakewood who share their stories with me, and those around the world who generously support our ministry and make it possible to bring hope to a world in need. I am grateful to all of those around the globe who follow our services on television, the Internet, and through the podcasts. You are all part of our Lakewood family.

I offer special thanks also to all the pastors across the country who are members of our Champions Network.

And last but not least, thanks to my wife, Victoria, and our children, Jonathan and Alexandra, who are my sources of daily inspiration, as well as to our closest family members who serve as day-to-day leaders of our ministry, including my brother, Paul, and his wife, Jennifer; my sister, Lisa, and her husband, Kevin; and my brother-in-law, Don, and his wife, Jackelyn.

CONTENTS

INTRODUCTION

There is a winner in you. You were created to be successful, to accomplish your goals, to leave your mark on this generation. You have greatness in you. The key is to get it out.

In this book, I've created eight principles that will help you reach your potential so that you can become all you were created to be. I've seen them work in my own life and in the lives of many others.

Too often we talk ourselves out of God's best. We allow doubts, fears, and discouraging things people have said to limit us and convince us to settle where we are. Negative voices always speak the loudest.

That's why I've titled this book, *You Can, You Will.* You have what it takes to win. You're talented enough. You're smart enough. You're experienced enough. You have the right personality and the right looks. You're the right nationality. You didn't get shortchanged. You're not lacking. You're fully equipped. You're the man or woman for the job.

This is your time. This is your moment. Put your

shoulders back. Hold your head up high. Walk with confidence. Winning is in your DNA, and it's about to come out in a greater way. You may have had some victories in the past, but you haven't seen anything yet.

As you put these principles into action, you will step into a new level of your destiny. You will discover talents you didn't know you had, and you will see God's blessing and favor in amazing ways.

Get ready! You can, you will!

YOU CAN
YOU WILL

CHAPTER ONE

Keep Your Vision in Front of You

A young man dreamed of being an actor, but in the early 1980s, he wasn't getting the big parts he wanted. Broke and discouraged, he drove his beat-up old car to the top of a hill overlooking the city of Los Angeles and did something unusual. He wrote himself a check for ten million dollars for "Acting services rendered."

This young man had grown up so poor his family lived in a Volkswagen van at one time. He put that check in his wallet and kept it there. When things got tough, he'd pull it out and look at it to remind himself of his dream.

A dozen years later, that same young man, the comedian Jim Carrey, was making fifteen million to twenty-five million a movie.

Studies tell us that we move toward what we consistently see. You should keep something in front of you, even if it's symbolic, to remind you of what you are believing for.

> *Keep something in front of you*

3

A businessman I met had a goal to build a new office for his company. He bought a brick, the same type of brick he wanted to use on his building. He keeps that brick on his desk.

Every time he sees it, he's moving toward his goal. It reminds him of what he's dreaming about. If you're single and you want to get married, put an empty photo album on your table. That's where you're going to put your wedding photos. When you see it, you're moving toward it.

You may not be reaching your highest potential, not because you don't have the faith, the talent, or the determination, but because you're not keeping the right things in front of you. All over your house, you should have pictures that inspire you, scripture verses that encourage you, mementoes that strengthen your faith. Maybe one of them is a key on your key ring for the new house you want to buy.

If somebody asks, "What's this extra key for?"

You say, "It is for the house that's on the way."

God will finish what He started

In the scripture, Zerubbabel wanted to rebuild the temple. He laid the foundation, but then the people came against him and made him stop. For ten years no work was done. One day the prophet Zechariah came by and told him to do something interesting. He said, "Go get the headstone." The headstone was the stone reserved to be the last piece of stone that went into the building. It was symbolic. It represented the finished product.

Why was it important for Zerubbabel to keep the headstone in front of him? Because every time he looked at the headstone, it was a reminder that God would finish what He started. When Zerubbabel was discouraged, when he was tired and thought it was impossible to finish the job, he would go over and look at the headstone. That was God saying to him, "I'm in control, I'm going to bring it to pass, just stay in faith."

Let me ask you: Do you have your headstone in front of you? Do you have something that represents the final piece to your dreams? My brother-in-law Kevin is a twin. Growing up, he loved having a twin sister. His dream was always to have twins. He and my sister Lisa tried to have a baby for a long time with no success. Lisa went through all the fertility treatments, including several surgeries, but still nothing.

They were very discouraged; it didn't look like it would ever happen. One day Kevin went out to get the mail, and there was a small package in the mailbox. The return address said it had come from Huggies. They hadn't ordered anything from Huggies. He opened it up and there were two diapers in it. They were sending out samples of their diapers as part of a promotion.

Kevin could have thrown away the package, thinking, "I don't need these—we don't have any children." But when he saw those two diapers something came alive on the inside. He took that as a sign from God. That was his headstone.

He ran in and told Lisa, "We just got the first diapers for our babies."

He wrote the date on those diapers and placed them on his desk at home. Month after month, he would see those diapers: in the morning before work, in the afternoon after coming home, and in the evening before he went to bed. When you see something long enough it gets into your subconscious mind. It eventually drops down into your spirit. That's when you know it's going to happen.

Several years later Kevin and Lisa received a phone call out of the blue asking if they would be interested in adopting a baby. They said, "Yes we would." The lady said, "How about adopting two? These are twin girls who are about to be born." Today Kevin and Lisa have their twins. They are teenagers now and as beautiful as can be.

Keep your vision in front of you

Are you believing for a child? Go buy a baby's outfit and hang it in your closet where you can see it every day. Keep your vision in front of you. A friend of mine who wanted a child decorated her whole baby's room, bought the bed and the stroller, spent all this time, money, and energy.

Her friends thought she was a little far out, preparing a baby's room with no baby on the way. But she understood this principle: What you keep in front of you, you are moving toward. A year went by and still no baby. Two years, no baby. Five years. Ten years.

She didn't get discouraged. She kept thanking God that her baby was on the way. All through the day when she'd walk by that baby's room, the seed was growing. It didn't look like anything was happening, but she was moving toward it. Twenty years later she had not one baby, but two. The stroller didn't work. The bed was out of date. She didn't care. She had her babies!

Is there something you see every day that reminds you of what you're believing for, something that inspires you, ignites your faith? Proverbs says, "Where there is no vision, the people perish." With no vision you'll get stuck. That's why

> Remember what you're believing for

many people have lost their passion. They don't have anything that reminds them of what they're dreaming about. If you're believing to move into a nicer house, find a picture of a house you like and put it on your bathroom mirror. Let that seed get into you.

If you're believing to get into a college, go buy the school's T-shirt and wear it around. Put the coffee mug with their logo on your counter. Every time you see that picture, that T-shirt, that baby's outfit, say under your breath: "Thank You, Lord, for bringing my dreams to pass. Thank You, Lord, that I'll become everything You created me to be."

I learned this from my father. He and my mother started Lakewood Church in 1959, in an old rundown feed store. They had ninety people. You know what my father called the church? Lakewood International Outreach Center.

There was a big blue sign outside. The sign cost more than

the building. The truth is, they weren't an international out-reach center. They were a small neighborhood church with ninety people. But every time my father drove up to that church and saw the sign, his vision was being increased. He was moving toward it.

When the ninety members saw the sign week after week, something was being birthed on the inside. Seeds of increase were taking root. Do you know what Lakewood is today? It is an international outreach center touching the world. Growing up, my father always kept a globe on his desk at home. At the old church there was a big world map on the wall. He put a globe behind him when he spoke. He always had the world on his mind. One year at the conference, people came from 150 countries. It looked like the United Nations.

What you keep in front of you, you're moving toward.

Release your faith in a big way

Now, don't have just a little vision. You're not inconveniencing God to believe big. In fact, it's just the opposite. When you believe to do great things, when you believe to set a new standard for your family, it pleases God.

Take the limits off and say, "I don't see a way, but God, I know You have a way, so I'm going to believe to have these twins. I will believe to start a business to impact the world. I will believe that my whole family will serve you. I will believe to get totally well."

When you release your faith in a big way it pleases God.

My father could have put on that sign just LAKEWOOD COM-MUNITY CHURCH. Nothing wrong with that, but God had put something bigger in his heart. He could have looked at the circumstances: "We're just ninety people. We don't have a lot of money. We don't have a nice building. We'll never do anything great." If he'd done that, we wouldn't be such a big church today.

It doesn't matter what it looks like in the natural; God is a supernatural God. He's not limited by your resources, by your environment, by your education, by your nationality. If you'll have a big vision, God will not only do what you're dreaming about, He will do more than you can ask or think.

A few years after my father went to be with the Lord and I stepped up to pastor the church, I had a desire to write a book. My dad had written many books, and they were all translated into Spanish. On the bookshelf I walk by at home every day, I had two copies of my dad's most popular book. One was in English. The other was in Spanish. I kept those books in front of me, knowing one day at the right time I would write a book. My dream was that it, too, would be translated into Spanish.

In my mind this seemed so far out. I never thought I could get up and minister, much less write a book. This was stretching my faith. A year went by, no book. Two years, three years, four years. It would have been easy to lose my passion and think it was never going to happen. But I had my father's books strategically placed on this bookshelf right outside my closet.

To get to the other parts of the house I had to go right by those two books. I saw them thousands and thousands of times. I didn't always consciously think about them, but even subconsciously I was moving toward writing my own. My faith was being released. Something on the inside was saying, "Yes, one day I'm going to write a book."

In 2004 I wrote my first book, *Your Best Life Now*. When the publisher read the manuscript they decided to publish it in English and Spanish at the same time. Normally they wait to see if anybody buys it first. But that's the way God is. His dream for your life is bigger than your own.

God will supersize your vision

I've found that whatever your vision is, God will supersize it. He will do more than you can ask or think. My vision was that my book would be so well received it would be translated into Spanish. But it was also translated into French, German, Russian, Swahili, Portuguese, and more than forty other languages.

If you keep the vision in front of you and don't get talked out of it, but just keep honoring God, being your best, thanking Him that it's on the way, God will supersize whatever you're believing for. He'll do exceedingly abundantly above and beyond.

Keep honoring God

I saw an article in the paper several years ago about a man who gave a university one hundred million dollars. I cut that article out and put it on my desk. Every time I see it I say, "God, you did it for a university, you can do it for a ministry."

I've got a big vision. We can reach a lot of people with an extra one hundred million. If you can accomplish your dreams in your own strength, talent, ability, and resources, then your dreams are too small. You don't need God's help with small dreams. Believe big. Your destiny is too great, your assignment too important, to have little goals, little dreams, little prayers.

Keep big things in front of you. A friend of mine feeds a million children a day. He and his wife support orphanages and feeding programs that touch a million kids every day. That's what I keep in front of me. "God, You did it for them, You can do it for us. Let our family impact millions of children."

In our kitchen at home, we have pictures of some of the children we sponsor through our partner World Vision. Every time we eat dinner, every time we pass by, we say, "God, let us make a bigger difference."

We're moving toward it. You may say, "Well, Joel, I can't even imagine that happening to me. I can't imagine me being that blessed." Don't worry—you won't be. If you don't have a vision for it, it's not going to happen. Without a vision you won't see God's best. You won't be the winner He wants you to be.

Use the power of your imagination

I know some things do seem far out or very unlikely, but don't ever say: "I can't imagine that." You see somebody really fit and energetic when you're trying to get back in shape, you may think: "I can't imagine looking like that." You may drive by a nice house and say, "I can't imagine living in this neighborhood." Or you may have thought: "I can't imagine publishing a book." "I can't imagine owning my own business." "I can't imagine being that successful."

The problem is you're being limited by your own imagination. You've got to change what you're seeing. Don't let negative thoughts paint those pictures. Use your imagination to see yourself accomplishing dreams, rising higher, overcoming obstacles, being healthy, strong, blessed, and prosperous.

I don't say this arrogantly, but I can imagine my books being published in every language, I can imagine somebody handing us that one-hundred-million-dollar check. I can imagine us feeding a million children a day. I can imagine living a long, healthy life. I can imagine my children superseding anything we've done.

Not only that, I can imagine you fulfilling your dreams. I can imagine you totally out of debt. I can imagine you healthy and strong. I can imagine you leading your company. I can imagine you blessing the world, being a history maker, setting a new standard for your family. Now I'm asking you not only to have it in your imagination, but to also keep something in front of you that reminds you of it.

A man I know works in the oil business. He started his company with just himself and one assistant. It grew and grew. He's always at our services, honoring God, giving, serving, and helping others. His company specializes in drilling for oil. He provides the crew and all the equipment.

He was spending all his time traveling around checking on the different sites.

One day he saw a competitor's employees boarding their own airplane. They were doing what he did in a fraction of the time. God dropped that dream in his heart, that he could have an airplane. This was so far out for him. He came from a family that lived paycheck to paycheck, barely getting by. He'd already broken out of the mold.

When his family members heard him talking about having an airplane, they thought he had lost his mind. They couldn't imagine it, but he could. Sometimes your family will not be your biggest cheerleader. They may not encourage you. You've got to listen to what God's telling you and not to what other people may tell you. People will try to talk you out of the dream in your heart.

Listen to what God's telling you

My friend went out and bought a model of the airplane he wanted and put it on his desk. People would come into his office and ask, "What's that plane for?" He would tell them, "That's my airplane. That's what I'm going to use to travel the country."

Year after year he kept that plane in front of him. One day the competitor that he'd seen flying around walked into his office. The older gentleman said, "I'm retiring. I'd like to sell you my airplane."

This man had a big, beautiful plane that could seat twelve people. My friend couldn't afford it. He was hoping to buy a little, used two-seater plane. He said, "I appreciate the offer, but I don't have those kinds of funds."

The competitor said, "Sure you do. You don't have to put any money down, just take over my monthly payments, and you can have the plane."

My friend got that big, beautiful plane for a fraction of the value, and today he flies all over the world. His company has taken off. He said, "Joel, God has done more than I ever imagined."

When you keep your vision in front of you, that's your faith being released. That's why the scripture uses such strong language that says people perish for lack of vision. That means dreams die when you don't have vision. If you can't see what God has put in your heart, then you'll miss the incredible things God wants to do.

Now, you may not need an airplane, but you may need to lose thirty pounds. Why don't you put up a picture of yourself thirty pounds lighter on your bathroom mirror? Every day when you see it, don't get depressed and think, "I wish I still looked like that. I wish I could fit into that dress."

Instead say, "Lord, thank you that I'm losing this weight. I'm healthy, whole, strong, in shape, energetic, attractive." Let that new image take root.

You may not be healthy today, but you need to keep something in front of you that says you're going to be healthy. Put up pictures of yourself when you were healthy and strong all over your house. Put up scripture verses; plan to take some trips to see your family. Check on that gym you want to join.

Don't you dare plan on dying. We need you, so plan on

living. Keep the right vision in front of you. You can. You will!

In the scripture, God promised Abraham that he would be the father of many nations. In the natural it was impossible. Abraham didn't have one child. He was eighty years old. But God didn't just give him the promise; God gave him a picture to look at.

God said, "Abraham, go out and look at the stars—that's how many descendants you will have." I've read where there are six thousand stars in the Eastern sky where he was. It's not a coincidence that there are six thousand promises in the scripture. God was saying, "Every promise that you can get a vision for, I will bring it to pass."

God told him also to look at the grains of sand at the seashore, because that was how many relatives he would have. Why did God give him a picture? God knew there would be times when it would look as if the promise would not come to pass, and Abraham would be discouraged and tempted to give up.

In those times, Abraham would go out at night and look up at the sky. When he saw the stars, faith would rise in his heart. Something would tell him, "It's going to happen, I can see it."

In the morning when his thoughts told him, "You're too old, it's too late, you heard God wrong," he would go down to the beach and look at the grains of sand. His faith would be restored.

Like Abraham, there will be times when it seems as if your dreams are not coming to pass. It's taking so long.

The medical report doesn't look good. You don't have the resources. Business is slow. You could easily give up.

But like Abraham, you've got to go back to that picture. Keep that vision in front of you. When you see the key to your new house, the outfit for your baby, the tennis shoes for when you're healthy, the picture frame for your spouse, the article inspiring you to build an orphanage, those pictures of what you're dreaming about will keep you encouraged.

God is saying to you what He said to Abraham: "If you can see it, then I can do it. If you have a vision for it, then I can make a way. I can open up new doors. I can bring the right people. I can give you the finances. I can break the chains holding you back."

Your dreams will fall into place

I read about a man named Conrad Hilton. He was the founder of the Hilton hotels. As a young man back in the 1930s, he saw an article about the Waldorf Astoria Hotel in New York City. The title of the article said it was the most famous hotel in the world. The article included big, beautiful pictures.

He'd never seen anything like that hotel. It was so grand, so magnificent. As he was reading the article, God put the dream in his heart to one day own that hotel. In the natural, it didn't seem possible. He could barely pay his rent. He didn't have any connections. The Depression was just ending.

Conrad Hilton could have said, "God, you have the wrong person, not me." Instead, he dared to let the seed take root. He cut out the picture of the big, beautiful Waldorf and put it under the glass on his desk. Every day he would see that picture for one year, two years, five years, ten years.

It did not look like his dream would happen, but he kept that vision in front of him. When he went to New York City, he walked around the Waldorf Astoria Hotel and prayed. He thanked God that it was his—but he did not tell anyone; he just let the dream take root.

Eighteen years later, his company was able to purchase nearly 250,000 shares of the Waldorf Corporation, and with that deal, he owned the most famous hotel in the world. Friends, what you keep in front of you, you're moving toward.

You may think it's too late—your dreams are too big, your obstacles too difficult—but God is still on the throne. He still has a way to bring them to pass. Just like with Mr. Hilton, God will do something big in your life. He will release His favor in a new way.

> God will do something big in your life

What you thought was over and done is still going to happen. When it looks impossible, like it's way over your head, God will suddenly cause things to fall into place, giving you favor, influence, and connections.

Don't stop believing. Every time you see your vision, you're moving toward it. Thank God that it's on the way.

If you'll do this God will supersize what you're dreaming about. He will take you further faster, opening doors that no man can shut, doing what medicine cannot do.

I believe and declare that every dream, every promise, every goal God put in your heart, He will bring to pass.

CHAPTER TWO

Run Your Race

There will always be people who try to squeeze you into their molds and pressure you into being who they want you to be. They may be good people. They may mean well, but the problem is they didn't breathe life into you. They didn't equip you or empower you. God did.

If you're going to become the winner you were created to be, you need to have a boldness. The second quality of a winner is that you run your race the way you want to run it.

You can't be insecure and you can't worry about what everyone thinks. You can't try to keep everyone happy. If you change with every criticism and play up to people, trying to win their favor, you'll go through life letting people manipulate you and pressure you into their boxes.

You have to accept the fact that you can't keep everyone happy. You can't make everyone like you. You will never win over every critic. Even if you changed and did everything they asked, some would still

You are living to please God

21

find fault. You're not really free until you're free from trying to please everyone. You're respectful, you're kind, but you're not living to please people, you're living to please God.

Every morning when you get up, you should search your heart. Know deep down that you're being true to who God called you to be. Then you won't have to look to the left or to the right. Just stay focused on your goals.

If people don't understand you, that is okay. If some get upset because you don't fit into their mold, don't worry about it. If you lose a friend because you won't let that person control you, then you didn't need them anyway, because that person was not a true friend.

If people talk about you, being jealous, critical, and trying to make you look bad, don't let that change you. You don't need their approval when you have God's approval.

If you will get free from what everyone else thinks and start being who you were created to be, you will rise to a new level. We spend too much time trying to impress people, trying to gain their approval, wondering what they're going to think if we take this job or wear a new outfit or move into a new neighborhood.

Instead of running our races, we often make decisions based on superficial things. I heard somebody say, at twenty years old we wonder what everybody thinks about us, and at forty years old we don't care what anybody thinks about us. Then, at sixty, we realize nobody was thinking about us.

Be true to who God wants you to be

I read an interesting report from a nurse who takes care of people close to death. She asked hundreds of patients facing death what their biggest regrets were. The number one regret was "I wish I had been true to who I was and not just lived to meet the expectations of others."

How many people today are not being true to who they are because they're afraid they may disappoint someone, they may fall out of their good graces, or they may not be accepted? I say this respectfully, but you can't live the life God wanted for you if you are trying to be who your parents want you to be, who your friends want you to be, or who your boss wants you to be. You have to be true to who God made you to be.

When my father went to be with the Lord, I had to accept the fact that the purpose for my life was different from my father's. His calling was to help bring down the denominational walls between churches, and he went around the world telling people about the fullness of the Spirit.

When I took over our church, I felt this pressure to be like my father, to fit into his mold. I thought I had to minister like him and run the church like him and go down the same road. But when I searched my heart, deep down I knew my calling was to plant a seed of hope, to encourage people, to let them know about the goodness of God.

It was a struggle, because I loved my father. Some people

had been at the church for forty years. I thought, "I can't be anything different. What would people think? They may not accept me, they may not like me." But one day I read a scripture about David. It said, "David fulfilled God's purpose for his generation."

I heard God say right down in my heart: "Joel, your dad fulfilled his purpose, now quit trying to be like him and go out and fulfill your purpose." When I heard that, it was as if a light turned on. I realized, "I don't have to be like my father. I don't have to fit into a certain mold; it's okay to run my race. I am free to be me."

After all God doesn't want you to be an imitation of someone else. You should be the original you were created to be. There is an anointing on your life, an empowerment. Not to be somebody else, but to be you. If you let people squeeze you into their molds and you bow down to their pressure to try to please your critics, it not only takes away your uniqueness, but it also lessens the favor on your life.

As our church started growing and more people started watching, the critics came out of the woodwork. People were saying, "He's not like his father. He doesn't have the experience. He's too young."

Even now, some say, "He's too much of this, or he's not enough of that." If you change with every criticism, you won't have a chance. I believe one reason God has promoted me is because I tuned out all the negative voices and I've done my best to stay true to who God made me to be.

I don't look to the left or to the right. I run my race. I don't try to compete with anyone else; I don't let people control me and go around feeling guilty because I don't fit into their boxes. I don't get upset because something negative is said about me. I look straight ahead and, as the apostle Paul said, I run with purpose in every step.

Run with a purpose

I learned early on that to please God I may have to disappoint a few people. There were several members who had been with the church for a long time, friends of the family for years, who were upset because I wasn't exactly like my father. I wouldn't let them squeeze me into their mold, so they left our church.

That was difficult for me. I wanted their approval. But looking back now, I realize had I let them pressure me into being who they wanted me to be, I would not be where I am today.

The scripture talks about those who loved the praise of people more than the praise of God. One of the tests we all have to pass is when someone in our lives that we respect and look up to—a boss, a friend, a

Love the praise of God

colleague, a relative—wants us to to go one direction, when we know in our hearts that we should take another path.

We don't want to hurt their feelings. We don't want to lose their friendship. We want their approval. But if we are to fulfill our destinies, we have to be strong. We have to have this attitude: "I want the praise of God more than the praise of people. I have an assignment. I have a purpose. I will become who God created me to be."

I've learned if you please God and stay true to what He's put in your heart, eventually you will have the praise of people. His favor, His anointing, His blessing, will cause you to excel.

You may lose a few friends early on. People may not understand why you don't take their advice. They may think you're making a big mistake, but later they'll see you walking in the fullness of your destiny.

You will see new opportunities, new relationships. God's favor on your life will increase if you quit worrying about what everyone thinks and do what God has put in your heart.

Everyone has an opinion. People will tell you how to run your life. They'll have opinions on what you should wear, what you should drive, how you should spend your money, and how you should raise your children.

If you try to please everyone, I can guarantee you one thing 100 percent: You'll be confused. You'll be frustrated. Life will be miserable.

I live by this motto: Everyone has a right to an opinion, and I have every right to not listen to it. If what others say doesn't match what God has put in your heart, let it go in one ear and out the other.

I heard about this man who fell into a pit, and while he was down there several people came by and offered their opinions.

The Pharisee said, "You deserve to be in the pit."

The Catholic said, "You need to suffer while you're in the pit."

The Baptist said, "If you'd been saved, you wouldn't have fallen into the pit."

The charismatic said, "Just confess I'm not in the pit."

The mathematician said, "Let me calculate how you fell into the pit."

The IRS agent said, "Have you paid taxes on that pit?"

The optimist said, "Things could be worse."

The pessimist said, "Things will get worse."

Everyone has an opinion. If you try to keep every person happy, the one person that will not be happy is you. Sometimes those who try to run your life and tell you what to do can't even run their own lives, much less yours.

It's fine to listen to opinions. It's great to receive advice, but you have to be secure enough in who God made you to be so that when something doesn't bear witness with your spirit, you'll have a boldness that says, "Thanks, but no thanks. I appreciate your advice, I value your opinion, but that's not for me."

You have to be aware especially of high-maintenance people. These people are almost impossible to keep happy. You've got to call them on their schedule, keep them cheered up, run their errands, and meet their demands. If not, they're upset and disappointed. And they'll do their best to make sure you feel guilty.

High-maintenance people are almost always controllers.

If you're not careful they'll squeeze you into their mold. They're not interested in you. They're interested in what you can do for them.

If you fall into the trap of always trying to please them, you will wear yourself out and constantly be frustrated. Years ago, I went out of my way to help this couple who were friends. They moved to another city, and I gave them money to help them move. I called and checked on them. If they needed anything I was always available.

Even so, I got the feeling from them that I was never doing enough. They were never satisfied. They always had a complaint. I had gone out of my way to be kind and generous, but they were constantly finding fault and trying to make me feel guilty.

One day I realized they were just high-maintenance people and I was not responsible for making them happy; I couldn't make them decide to like me. I had to run my race and not let them steal my joy. That was a great day in my life!

Your time is too valuable to worry about pleasing everyone else or making them happy. I know people who spend more time worrying about what others think about them than they do focusing on their own dreams and goals. You've got to get free from that.

If you're going to do anything great in life—if you're to be a great teacher, a great businessperson, a great athlete, a great parent, and a great winner—not everyone will cheer you on. I would love to tell you that all of your family, friends, and coworkers will celebrate you, but unfortunately that's not the case.

Some won't be able to handle your success. If you were where you were ten years ago, they would have no problem with you. But as you succeed, as God pours out His favor, some will be jealous. Some will find fault.

Don't be surprised if a family member or a relative tries to discredit you, belittle you, or won't give you the time of day, or maybe a friend you've been good to for years won't understand you. Let that bounce off you like water off a duck's back. If you don't then you'll start changing, being defensive, thinking that you've got to prove to them that you're really okay. What you're doing is letting them squeeze you into their mold.

Your destiny is too great to get distracted trying to win over people who are never going to like you. Don't take it personally. It's not about you. It's about the favor God put on your life. It stirs up the jealousy in them.

> *Your destiny is too great to get distracted*

Until they deal with it, nothing you can do will change it. You might as well shake it off and run your race, because no matter how good you are to them they will still find fault. No matter how much you try to show them kindness, they will still find some reason to be critical.

It's like this country grandfather I heard about who took his grandson to town on a donkey. He started off letting his grandson ride the donkey as he walked alongside. Somebody passed by and said, "Look at that selfish boy making that old man walk."

The grandfather heard it and took the boy off. Then he rode the donkey as his grandson walking by his side. Somebody came along and said, "Look at that man making that little boy walk while he rides."

Hearing that, the grandfather pulled the little boy up with him, and they both started riding the donkey. In a few minutes, another person said, "How cruel of you and the boy to place such a heavy load on the donkey."

By the time they got to town, the grandfather and grandson were carrying the donkey!

The point is that no matter what you do, you will never please everybody. You may as well accept the fact that even when you do the best you can, some will find fault with you, and that's okay. They have a right to have their opinions, and you have a right to ignore them.

Take control of your happiness

Too many people sacrifice their own happiness to keep someone else happy. They've got to stop by their friend's house and say hello, because they don't want to upset the friend. They stay late at night in the office, because if they don't their boss may be unhappy. They've got to loan this friend money, because the friend is in trouble again. If they don't meet all the demands and fix this person, rescue this person, solve this person's problem, then they'll fall out of somebody's good grace, and that somebody won't understand and will get upset.

But God did not call you to keep everyone happy. It's good to be loving, kind, and generous, but you are not responsible for the happiness of others. You are responsible for your own happiness.

You may feel that if you don't meet all their demands and needs, if you don't rescue them or loan them money, then they'll be angry with you.

But if that's the case, maybe it's time for them to be unhappy instead of you. If they get mad, they're manipulators. They are using you.

Your time is too valuable to go through life letting people control you and make you feel guilty if you don't come running every time they call. The easy thing is to just give in and keep bailing them out, so you don't make any waves.

But as long as you rescue them and you're there to cheer them up and keep them all fixed up, you're not really helping them. You're a crutch. Because of you, they don't have to deal with the real issues. You're enabling their dysfunction.

The only way these dependent people will get the help they need is for you to stop being their crutch. Don't come running every time they have an "emergency."

Put your foot down and say, "I love you, but I'm not going to let you control me. I love you, but I'm jumping every time you call. I love you, but I refuse to feel guilty if I don't meet all your demands."

If people are controlling you, it's not their fault, it's your fault. You have to set some boundaries. Quit allowing them to call you all hours of the day to dump their problems on you. That's why we have voice mail!

Quit caving in to them every time they throw a fit. Ignore it. Quit loaning them money every time they make poor choices. Don't take on a false sense of responsibility. You are not the savior of the world. We already have a Savior. You're not supposed to keep everyone happy or fixed. If you take on that job, the one person who will not be happy is you.

Years ago I knew this man who was always having problems paying his rent. My heart went out to him, and I helped him again and again. Every other month he would claim that something had come up that kept him from making his payment. After about the fifth emergency request for rent money, I started to wise up.

He told me a client hadn't paid him. He told me the check was in the mail but hadn't arrived. He also claimed a relative had become sick, and he'd been called out of town. His excuses went on and on.

At the end of another long, sad story, he said, "Now what are we going to do?"

I thought to myself, "We're not going to do anything because this is not my problem. This is your problem, and I'm not going to feel guilty because you keep making poor choices."

I believe I'd still be helping him today five years later if I had not put my foot down. When you refuse to keep helping people like that, you force them to look inside and take responsibility. A lot of times we do things out of guilt, because we think we'll feel bad if we don't help overly dependent or manipulative people.

But if they're not taking responsibility for their own lives, then you're not helping them—you're hurting them. They need to deal with their own issues like most people. When you back away, it will force them to change.

Don't play the puppet

I've learned to recognize that some people are always having a crisis. Every other day they have an emergency or they are in desperate need of something. It's good to help people who are in real need. But if someone comes to you a dozen times, or year after year, and it seems the emergencies never stop, you need to recognize that's a manipulator.

It's like they have you as their puppet. They know if they pull one string you'll feel guilty, or another string and you'll bail them out, or another and you'll stay late and do a work or school project for them.

If someone is playing you like a puppet, it's time to cut the strings. No more letting them make you feel guilty. No more will you come running. You may feel you'll lose their friendship if you refuse to help them, but that feeling is your wake-up call. God just met your need. He just closed that door for you. The truth is if someone becomes upset because you won't meet unreasonable demands, then that person is not your friend. That person is a manipulator. The sooner you break free, the better off you'll be.

Are you doing too much for other people and not enough

| *Keep yourself happy* |

for yourself? Are you so good-hearted that you're sacrificing your happiness to keep everyone around you happy? Understand this: Your first priority is to keep yourself happy.

If you are giving all the time and not receiving anything in return, then you need to examine your relationships. They are out of balance. You shouldn't have to constantly meet the demands and needs of your friends out of fear of being rejected by them. You should be able to tell them no without feeling guilty.

If they give you the cold shoulder and won't speak to you, then they're not really friends, they're manipulators. The sooner you make a change, the better off you will be.

Don't waste twenty years playing up to people, trying to meet all their demands, when the truth is they're not interested in you, they're interested in what you can do for them.

The best thing you can do is to cut the puppet strings. You don't have time to play games, get entangled, or become distracted trying to keep everybody happy. You have a destiny to fulfill. Be bold, take charge of your life, and pursue the dreams God has placed in your heart.

When I was growing up, my grandfather would buy a new car every two years, and he would give his old car to one of us grandchildren. He was very generous. My junior year he gave me his Buick LeSabre. A friend of mine on the basketball team had a car as well. We decided to carpool. I'd come pick him up for school one week and he'd pick me up the next week. He lived fifteen minutes in the opposite direction of the school.

I'd have to go get him and come all the way back. I didn't mind. I drove one week then he drove the next. We did this for a month or so with no problems, but then his car broke down one week, so I had to drive again. I had to take another of his weeks because his brother needed the car. Then something else came up and he missed another turn. It got to where I was driving all the time. I really didn't mind, but he wasn't very grateful; he acted like I owed it to him.

One day I got my nerve up and asked him if he was planning on ever driving again. He told me how he was trying to keep the mileage down on his car and basically that I needed to keep picking him up. He acted like he was doing me a favor to let him ride in my car.

I did what I'm asking you to do. I kept a big smile and told him very politely that I wasn't able to come get him anymore. You would have thought I'd told him his life was ending. He gave me the biggest guilt trip and tried to make me feel like I was such a selfish person. He hardly spoke to me after that.

I thought, "That's fine with me. If you're only my friend if I meet your demands and cater to your every need, then good riddance. I don't need friends like that. Go find somebody else to control, because you're not controlling me."

I don't mind being good to people, but I do mind being used.

If you allow it, people will run your life. They'll tell you what to do, where to go, how to dress, and how to spend your money. It's good to get free from addictions, free from anxiety, and free from depression, but one of the greatest freedoms is to get free from controlling people.

Quit letting others pressure you into being something that you're not. Quit living on eggshells because you don't want to fall out of their favor. Quit feeling afraid that if you don't perform perfectly—call on cue, come running when they ask—they'll be upset. Here's my message: Let them be upset. If you spend your life trying to please everyone and letting them control you, they may be happy but you'll end up missing your destiny. I'd rather please God and have some people upset with me than please people and have God upset with me.

Fly with those who lift you up and thrust you forward

A pilot friend of mine told me there are four main principles to master when flying airplanes: lift, thrust, weight, and drag. You have to take all these into account to make sure the plane will fly.

It struck me that these same principles apply to specific types of people. There are some who lift you, brighten your day, cheer you up, and make you feel better about yourself. You meet them and you have a spring in your step. They're a lift. Then there are people who thrust you. They inspire you, motivate you, challenge you to move forward and pursue your dreams. The third group are weights. They pull you down, dump their problems on you, so that you leave feeling heavier, negative, discouraged, and worse than you did before.

Finally, there are those who are a drag. They've always got a sad song. The dishwasher broke. The goldfish died. They didn't get invited to a party. They're stuck in a pit. They expect you to cheer them up, fix their problems, and carry their loads.

We all encounter people from each of these four groups. You have to make sure you're spending the majority of your time with lifters and thrusters. If you're only hanging out with weights and drags, it will keep you from becoming everything you were created you to be.

Some people have a perpetual problem. They always have a sad song. If you allow them, they'll use you as a trash can to dump all their garbage in. You spend an hour with them and you feel like you've run a marathon. They're energy suckers. You leave them feeling drained and worn out.

You cannot continue to deal with them day after day if you expect to reach your highest potential. You won't lift off. You won't thrust forward into the good things God has in store if you're weighted down, letting people dump their loads on you. They'll make you discouraged and drain your energy.

It's hard enough just to keep yourself cheered up. You're not responsible for their happiness. Sure, there are times when we need to sow a seed and have a listening ear and take time to love people back into wholeness. But that should be for a season and not an ongoing drama. You shouldn't spend every day listening to friends complain about their spouses or their neighbors.

If you do, your life will be like an episode of *Guiding*

Light, *Jersey Shore*, and *The Real Housewives of Beverly Hills* all put together. You have enough drama in your life without listening to everyone else's drama. You can't allow someone to put that negativity in you day after day if you expect to soar.

You need to evaluate the people you're spending time with. Are they lifters and encouragers? Do they make you feel better? Do you leave their company feeling inspired and happier, or are they dragging you down, making you feel drained, and sapping your energy?

When I was in my early twenties, this young lady cut my hair. She was as nice as could be. She had a good heart, but she was so negative. Every time I went she told me all of her problems. This went on month after month and year after year. She claimed the shop owners weren't treating her right and they made her work extra hours. She had a sister who was causing her problems. She didn't know if she could pay her rent, and her father wasn't doing well.

Look for encouragers in your life

Every time I left her shop I felt depressed. She was very convincing. I did my best to encourage her. I prayed with her. I gave her money. I sent her customers. But it was never enough.

One day I realized what I'm telling you: "I cannot get to where I'm going with her in my life. I love her. I will pray for her. But I cannot fulfill my destiny with that weight on me month after month."

I made a change. It was difficult. I don't like to hurt

feelings, but I realized my assignment is too important and my time is too valuable to let people continually pull me down.

You may have to make changes where you do business, where you play ball, or where you work out. You may have to change the phone calls you take. You shouldn't spend an hour on the phone every night listening to somebody's woes or hearing their sad songs. Put an end to it. Be kind, be respectful, but you don't need that weight going into you.

You need to be around lifters, thrusters, people who inspire you and motivate you. That's why so many are drawn to our ministry. There are enough weights, enough drags. I'm going to push you forward. If you get around me, I'm going to lift you, encourage you, inspire you. I'm going to do my best to leave you better than you were before.

You may work around people who are a drag. You don't have a choice. Or you may go to school with people who are a weight. They're negative and sour. Here's the key: Before you leave home, get prayed up, praised up, encouraged.

Set your mind that it's going to be a great day. You can't go into that negative environment in neutral. You've got to go in already filled up, already encouraged. Don't go with your guard down, stressed out from the traffic, worried about the deadline, or listening to depressing news reports.

If you're not on the offensive, then the weights and the drags will pull you down. Maybe you've got a twenty-minute drive on the way to work or school. Put on some good praise music. Get your spirit man built up. Build up a grateful attitude. Thank God for what He's done. Put on a good teaching DVD, something that inspires and motivates you. Talk to yourself the right way: "This is going to be a great day. I'm strong in the Lord. I've got the favor of God. I can do all things through Christ. Something good is going to happen to me."

That's how you'll stay strong and not let the weights and drags pull you down. You've got to build up a resistance.

What happens if you live with someone that's a weight? Perhaps you're married to a weight or a drag. Now I'm getting real! You've got to do the same thing: Take extra doses of praise, encouragement, and inspiration. Stay filled up.

While they're changing, don't let them steal your joy. Some people don't want to be happy. They're always in the pits. Living with them is like living in the pits. You've got to have the attitude: "If you don't want to be happy, that's fine, but you're not going to keep me from being happy. If you want to stay in the pits, that's your choice, but I'm not getting in the pits with you."

Take responsibility for your own happiness. Don't let their issues sour your life. Pray for them, be respectful, but don't become codependent. Don't let their problems become your problems. Don't let them keep you from your destiny. It's time to break free.

Is there something keeping you from being happy? Are you allowing somebody to control you or make you feel guilty if you don't meet all their demands? Cut the puppet strings. Set some boundaries. Don't miss your destiny trying to please everyone.

God did not call you to be unhappy. He does not want

you to waste your life trying to keep someone else happy. Be kind. Be compassionate, but run your own race. Remember, you don't need people's approval, you have God's approval.

Be secure enough in who you are that you don't live to please people. As long as you're doing what God has put in your heart, you don't need to look to the left or the right. Stay focused on your goals, and God will get you where you're supposed to be.

CHAPTER THREE

Expect Good Things

Our expectations set the limits for our lives. If you expect little, you're going to receive little. If you don't anticipate things to get better, then they won't. But if you expect more favor, more good breaks, a promotion, and an increase, then you will see new levels of favor and success.

Expect more favor

Every morning when you wake up, you should declare, "Something good is going to happen to me today." You have to set the tone at the beginning of each day. Then all through the day you should have this attitude of expectancy.

Like a little child waiting to open a gift, you should be on the lookout, thinking, "I can't wait to see what's going to happen"—not passive, but actively expecting.

Too many people drag around, thinking, "Nothing good ever happens to me." Instead, start looking for good breaks. Expect to be at the right place at the right time. Expect your dreams to come to pass. Expect to be a winner.

Don't walk into a room anticipating people to not like you. Don't go to the store believing that you won't find what you need. Don't interview for a job assuming not to get it. Your expectation is your faith at work. When you expect good breaks, expect people to like you, or expect to have a great year, then you're releasing your faith. That's what allows good things to happen.

But your expectations work in both directions. If you get up in the morning and expect it to be a lousy day and expect no breaks and expect people to be unfriendly, then you'll draw that in. Your faith is working. The problem is you're using it in the wrong direction.

Upgrade your expectations

A young person told me he was concerned about taking his final exams. He had studied and prepared, but he was very worried because every time he took an important test, he stressed out and couldn't remember what he had studied. He always ended up doing poorly.

"Joel, would you pray for me, because I know it's going to happen again," he said.

He was already expecting to fail. I shared with him this principle and told him he was anticipating the wrong things. I said, "You've got to change your expectations. All through the day say to yourself: 'I'm going to do great on this test. I'm going to remember everything that I've studied. I'm going to stay calm and in peace.'"

He came back a few weeks later and said that was the best he had ever done on one of his exams.

Let me ask you, what are you expecting? Big things, little things, or nothing at all? It's easy to anticipate the worst. But if you'll switch over into faith and expect the best—to excel, to accomplish your dreams—then you'll draw in blessings and favor.

Some people have had a negative mind-set so long they don't realize they're doing it. It's just natural to them. They assume the worst, and they usually get it. They expect people to be unfriendly, and people usually are.

I know a lady who has been through a lot of negative things in her life, and it was like she was on autopilot. She expected people to hurt her, and they usually did. She expected people to be dishonest, and they usually were. She expected to get laid off from her job, and eventually she did.

Her expectations were drawing in all the negative. One day she learned this principle and she started anticipating different things. She waited for the best instead of the worst. She expected to get good breaks. She expected people to like her. Today it's totally turned around. She's living a victorious life.

You may have had disappointments and unfair situations, but don't make the mistake of living in a negative frame of mind. Instead of expecting more of the same, start expecting it to turn around. Don't think you will barely get by; know that you will excel. Don't expect to be overcome. Expect to be the overcomer.

You may not always feel like it, but when you get up each day you need to remind yourself that you are more than a conqueror. Your greatest victories are still out in front of you. The right people, the right opportunities, the right breaks are already in your future.

Now go out and be excited about the day, expecting things to change in your favor. Your attitude should be: "I'm expecting good breaks, to meet the right people, to see an increase in business, to get my child back on track, and for my health to improve. I'm expecting to be at the right place at the right time."

Don't let negative expectations limit your life

A young man told me: "I don't want to expect too much. That way if it doesn't happen I won't go to bed all disappointed."

That's no way to live. If you're not expecting increase, promotion, or good breaks, you're not releasing your faith. Faith is what causes God to act. If you expect a break and it doesn't happen, don't go to bed disappointed. Go to bed knowing you're one day closer to seeing it come to pass. Get up the next morning and do it again.

Winners develop this third undeniable quality of expecting good things. You can't be in neutral and hope to reach your full potential or have God's best. It's not enough to not expect anything bad; you have to aggressively expect good things. Are you expecting your dreams to come to pass? Do you expect this year will be better than last year? Are you expecting to live a long, healthy, blessed life? Pay attention to what you're expecting. Maybe you have a desire to get married. Don't go around thinking: "I'll never meet anyone. It's been so long, and I'm getting too old." Instead, expect to be at the right place at the right time.

Believe that divine connections will come across your path. Believe that the right person will be attracted to you.

"What if I do that and nothing happens?"

What if you do it and something does happen? I can tell you nothing will happen if you don't believe.

David said in the Psalms: "Surely goodness and mercy will follow me all the days of my life." In the past you may have had disappointments and setbacks following you around, but you need to let go of what didn't work out. Let go of every mistake, and let go of every failure.

Expect goodness and mercy to follow you wherever you go. It's good to look back some-times and just say, "Hey, good-

> Goodness and mercy will follow you

ness. Hey, mercy. How are you doing back there?"

Some people don't realize that they're always looking for the next disaster, looking for the next failure, or looking for the next bad break. Change what you're looking for. Start looking for goodness, mercy, favor, increase, and promotion. That's what should be following you around.

One definition of hope is "happy anticipation of something good." If you're anticipating something good, it's going to bring you joy. It will give you enthusiasm. When you're expecting your dreams to come to pass, you'll go out each day with a spring in your step. But if you're not anticipating anything good, then you'll drag through life with no passion.

I don't say this arrogantly, but I expect people to like me. Maybe I'm naïve, but if I am, do me a favor and leave me in my ignorance. When I go somewhere, I don't have all these walls up. I'm not defensive, insecure, intimidated, or thinking, "They're not going to like me. They're probably talking about me right now."

I expect people to be friendly. I believe that when people turn on my television program they can't turn me off. I think when people see my book in the stores they'll be drawn to it.

I'm talking about having an attitude of expecting good things. You need to get your *expecter* out. Maybe you haven't used it for six years. You need to start expecting greater things.

There are new mountains to climb, and new horizons to explore. Expect to rise higher. Expect to overcome every obstacle. Expect doors to open. Expect favor at work, favor at home, favor at the grocery store, and favor in your relationships.

Remember the good

When you've been through hurts, disappointments, and failures, you have to guard your mind. Be careful what you allow to play in your thoughts all day. Your memory is very powerful.

You can be driving in your car and remember a tender moment with your child. It may have happened five years ago: a hug, a kiss, or something funny they did. But when you remember the moment, a smile comes to your face. You'll feel the same emotions, the same warmth and joy, just as if it were happening again.

On the other hand you could be enjoying the day; everything is fine, but then you start remembering some sad event when you weren't treated right or something unfair happened. Before long you'll be sad, discouraged, and without passion.

What made you sad? Dwelling on the wrong memories. What made you happy? Dwelling on the right memories. Research has found that your mind will naturally gravitate toward the negative. One study discovered that positive and negative memories are handled by different parts of the brain. A negative memory takes up more space because there's more to process. As a result, you remember negative events more than positive events.

The study said that a person will remember losing fifty dollars more than he'll remember gaining fifty dollars. The negative effect has a greater impact, carrying more weight than the positive.

I've experienced this myself. I can walk off the platform after speaking and a hundred people might tell me, "Joel, that was great today. I really got something out of it." But I'll be more likely to remember just one person who says, "I didn't understand it. That didn't do anything for me."

In the old days, the negative comment would be all I'd think about. I'd play it over and over in my mind. That's human nature. That's how negative memories are stored in our brain. The bad takes up more space than the good.

Tune into good memories

Knowing this, you have to be proactive. When negative memories come back to the movie screen of the mind, many people pull up a chair, get some popcorn, and watch it all again. They'll say: "I can't believe they hurt me, that was so wrong."

Instead, remember this: That's not the only movie playing. There's another channel that is not playing back your defeats, your failures, or your disappointments. This channel features your victories, your accomplishments, and the things you did right.

The good-memory channel plays back the times you were promoted, you met the right person, you bought a great house, and your children were healthy and happy.

Instead of staying on that negative channel, switch over to your victory channel. You will not move forward into better days if you're always replaying the negative things that have happened.

We've all been through loss, disappointments, and bad breaks. So those memories will come to mind most often. The good news is you have the remote control. Just because the memory comes up doesn't mean you have to dwell on it. Learn to change the channel.

A couple of years after my father died, I stopped by my mother's house to pick up something. Nobody was home. As I walked through the den, I immediately began to recall the night my father died. He had a heart attack in that very room. I could see him lying on the floor.

By the time I got there on the day he died, the paramedics were shocking him, trying to get his heart to restart. That whole night played out in my mind, and I could feel the same emotions.

Then I did what I'm asking you to do. I said, "No thanks, I'm not going there. I'm not reliving that night. I'm not feeling those same sad and depressing emotions."

I chose to change the channel. I started remembering all the great times we had together: the times we laughed and had fun, and traveled the world. I focused on the time we went down the Amazon River, and the times my father played with our son Jonathan.

There was another channel. I just had to switch to it. Do you need to start changing the channel? Are you reliving every hurt, disappointment, and bad break? As long as you're replaying the negative, you will never fully heal. It's like a scab that's starting to get better, but it will only get worse if you pick at it.

Emotional wounds are the same way. If you're always reliving your hurts and watching them on the movie screen of your mind—talking about them, and telling your friends—that's just reopening the wound.

You have to change the channel. When you look back over your life, can you find one good thing that has happened? Can you remember one time where you know it was the hand of God, promoting you, protecting you, and healing you? Switch over to that channel. Get your mind going in a new direction.

Stay tuned to good things

A reporter asked me not long ago what my biggest failure has been, my biggest regret. I don't mean to sound arrogant, but I don't remember what my biggest failure was. I don't dwell on that. I'm not watching that channel.

We all make mistakes. We all do things we wish we had done differently. You can learn from your mistakes, but you're not supposed to keep them in the forefront of your mind. You're supposed to remember the things you did right: The times you succeeded. The times you overcame the temptation. The times you were kind to strangers.

Some people are not happy because they remember every mistake they've made since 1927. They've got a running list. Do yourself a big favor and change the channel. Quit dwelling on how you don't measure up and how you just should have been more disciplined, should have stayed in school, or should have spent more time with your children.

You may have fallen down, but focus on the fact that you got back up. You're here today. You may have made a poor choice, but dwell on your good choices. You may have some weaknesses, but remember your strengths. Quit focusing on what's wrong with you and start focusing on what's right with you. You won't ever become all you were created you to be if you're against yourself. You have to retrain your mind. Be disciplined about what you dwell on.

Several years ago, I was playing basketball with our son Jonathan. We've played one-on-one for years. For the first time, he beat me, fair and square, 15–14. I gave him a high five. Then I told him he was grounded!

During the game at one point Jonathan dribbled around me and went up for a shot. I came out of nowhere, timed it just right, and blocked his shot. I swatted the ball away and it went flying into the bushes.

I felt like an NBA star. A couple days later, we went to the gym to play with some friends. Jonathan said, "Dad, tell everybody what happened the other night."

I said, "Oh, yeah, Jonathan went up for this shot, and I must have been this high in the air and I blocked it, and it was something else."

He said, "No, Dad, I meant tell them how I beat you for the first time!"

What's funny is, I didn't remember my defeat, I remembered my victory. The first thing that came to my mind wasn't that I lost the game to him, but the fact that I did something good. It's because I've trained my mind to remember the right things.

For many people it's just the opposite. They won the game, but they remember all the mistakes they made. They never feel good about themselves. They're always focused on something they didn't do good enough.

It's all in how you train your mind. It depends on what channel you're watching. Don't make the mistake of remembering what you should forget, whether it's your hurts, your disappointments, or your failures. Don't forget what you should remember—your victories, your successes, and the hard times you overcame.

Collect the positives in your past

In the Old Testament, God commanded His people to have certain feasts and certain celebrations. One of the main reasons was so they would remember what He had done. Several times a year they would stop what they were doing so everybody could take off. They would celebrate how God brought them out of slavery and how God defeated their enemies and how He protected them. They were required to remember.

In another place it talks about how they put down what they called "memorial stones." These were big stones. Today, we would call them historical markers. The stones reminded them of specific victories. Every time they would go by certain stones they would recall an event. "This stone was for when we were brought out of slavery. This stone is for when our child was healed. This stone is for how God provided for our needs." Having these memorial stones helped them to keep God's deeds fresh in their memories.

In the same way, you should have your own memorial stones. When you look back over your life, you should remember not when you failed, not when you went through a divorce, not when your business went down, not when you lost that loved one, not when the boss did you wrong. That's remembering what you're supposed to forget.

You need to switch over to the other channel. Remember when you met the love of your life, remember when your child was born, remember when you got that new position, remember when the problem suddenly turned around, remember the peace you felt when you lost a loved one.

Remember the strength you had in that difficult time. It looked dark. You didn't think you'd see another happy day again, but God turned it around and gave you joy for mourning, beauty for ashes,

> *Remember past strength*

and today you're happy, healthy, strong. We should all have our own memorial stones.

My mother recently marked the thirty-first anniversary of her victory over cancer. Thirty-one years ago, the doctors gave her a few weeks to live, but another year just went by, and she's still healthy and whole. That's a memorial stone.

Another one for me is December 1, 2003, when Mayor Lee Brown handed us the key to our new church building in Houston. That facility is a memorial stone. I also remember when I walked into a jewelry store and met Victoria for the first time. God answered her prayer. I mean *my* prayer!

I put up another memorial stone in remembrance of the fact that when my father died, I didn't know how to minister, but God gave me the grace to step up and pastor the church.

That's what I'm constantly remembering—good things. My question to you is: Do you have any memorial stones out? What you remember will have a great impact on what kind of life you live. If you're remembering your failures, your disappointments, and your hurts, that will keep you stuck in a rut.

If you'd just change what you're remembering—start remembering your successes, your victories, and the times you've overcome—that will allow you to step into new levels of favor. You may be in tough times, facing challenges, but when you remember the right things, you won't be saying, "This problem is too big. This sickness is going to be the end of me." Instead, you'll be saying, "God, you did it for me once, and I know you can do it for me again."

This is what David did when he was about to face Goliath, a giant twice his size. He could have focused on how big Goliath was and how Goliath had more experience, more training, and more weapons. All that would have done is discourage him.

The scripture says, "David remembered that he had killed a lion and a bear with his own hands." What was he doing? Remembering his victories. David could have remembered that his brothers mistreated him and his father disrespected him. There were negative things in his past, just like with all of us. But David understood this principle: Dwelling on defeats, failures, and unfair situations will keep you stuck.

He chose to dwell on his victories, and he rose above that challenge and became who God created him to be. You may feel like you're up against a giant. The way you're going to stay encouraged and the way you will have the faith to overcome is to do like David.

Instead of dwelling on how impossible it is and how you'll never make it, remember your victories all through the day. Get your memorial stones out. "Lord, thank you for that time when all the odds were against me, but You turned it around. God, I remember when You promoted me, vindicated me, made my wrongs right."

Rehearse your victories. Remembering the good things will make you strong.

Relive the joy

In 2007, a young lady named Rachel Smith won the Miss USA beauty pageant. She's a very bright girl who has traveled the world helping underprivileged children. Later that year, she competed in the Miss Universe pageant. As she was walking out on the stage, during the evening gown competition, she lost her footing on the slick floors and fell flat on her back. Millions of people around the world were watching on television. She was so embarrassed. She got up as quickly as she could and kept a smile on her face. The audience wasn't very forgiving. There were jeers and laughs and boos. It was very humiliating.

In spite of that fall, Rachel made it to the top five. She had to go up and answer a question randomly chosen from a hat. She walked out again to the same spot where she had fallen just a few minutes early. She pulled a question out of the hat with millions of people watching. The question was: "If you could relive and redo any moment of your life over again, what moment would that be?"

She had just experienced the most embarrassing moment of her life twenty minutes earlier. How many of us would have said, "I'd like to relive that moment when I fell on this stage. I'd like to do that over again."

But without missing a beat she said, "If I could relive anything again, I would relive my trip to Africa working with the orphans, seeing their beautiful smiles, feeling their warm hugs."

Instead of reliving a moment of embarrassment, a moment of pain, Rachel chose to replay a moment of joy, where she was making a difference, where she was proud of herself. We all fall down in our lives. We all make mistakes. We all have embarrassing, unfair moments.

You can be sure those images will replay again and again on the movie screen of your mind. You've got to do as Rachel Smith did: Change the channel and put on your victories, put on your successes, put on your accomplishments.

God performed miracle after miracle for the Israelites. He supernaturally brought them out of slavery. He sent all these plagues on their enemies. Even though the Israelites were living next door, the plagues did not affect them. When they came to a dead end at the Red Sea, with Pharaoh and his army chasing them, it might have looked like their lives were all over, but the water parted.

They went through the sea on dry ground. God gave them water out of a rock, and He led them by the cloud by day and the pillar of fire by night. But in spite of all of this they never made it into the Promised Land. Psalm 78 tells why. It says, "They forgot what God had done, they didn't remember the amazing miracles He had shown them and their ancestors."

When you forget what you should be remembering, it can keep you out of your Promised Land. The Israelites became discouraged, started complaining, and asked Moses, "Why did you bring us out here to die in the desert?"

When they faced an enemy, they thought, "We don't have a chance." They already had seen God's goodness in amazing ways. They had seen God do the impossible, but because they forgot about it, they were afraid, worried, and negative. It kept them from their destiny.

God can do it again

Are you forgetting what God has done for you? Have you let what once was a miracle become ordinary? It doesn't excite you anymore. You need to look back over your life and remember your victories, big and small. You'll know if God did it for you once, He can do it for you again.

You may get discouraged and think, "I don't see how I'll ever get out of this problem. Or I'll never get out of debt. Or I'll never get well." But when that happens, go back and remember the Red Seas God has parted for you. Remember the enemies He's delivered you from. Remember the battles He's fought, and the restoration, the vindication, and the favor He's shown.

Every one of us can look back and see the hand of God on our lives. God has opened doors that should have never opened for you, just as He did for the Israelites. He's helped you accomplish things you never could have accomplished on your own. He's brought you out of difficulties that you thought you'd never survive. He's protected, promoted, and given you opportunity.

The key to staying encouraged so you can see God open new doors and turn negative situations around is to never forget what He has done. In fact, the scripture says, "We should tell our children and our grandchildren." We should pass down stories of the goodness of God.

See the hand of God in your life

In the Old Testament, we read a lot about the staffs people carried around with them. They weren't just walking sticks, or something to keep wild animals away. They were more significant than that.

Back in those days, people were nomadic. They were always on the move. They didn't keep records with papers and computer files like we have today. Instead, they etched records of important events and dates on their walking staffs.

That was their way of keeping personal records. They'd etch notations such as, "On this date we defeated the Amalekites. On this date my son was born. On this date God brought us out of slavery. On this date God gave us water out of the rock."

Their walking staffs provided a record of their history with God. When Moses parted the Red Sea, what did he do? He held up his staff. He was saying, "God, we thank You for all You've done in the past. We remember that You've delivered us time and time again."

Moses was remembering the great things God had done. When David went out to face Goliath, he didn't just take his slingshot. The scripture says he took his staff. On that staff, no doubt, he had etched, "On this date I killed a lion with my bare hands. On this date I killed a bear. On this date Samuel anointed me as king."

David took his staff to remind him that God had helped him in the past. I can imagine just before he went out to fight, he ran over and read it one more time. That gave him the final boost. His attitude was, "God, You did it for me back then, so I know You can do it for me now."

Are you facing giants today? Does your problem look too big? Do your dreams seem impossible? You need to get your staff out. Instead of going around discouraged, and thinking it's never going to work out, start dwelling on your victories. Start thinking about how you killed the lion and bear in your own life. Start remembering how far God has brought you.

Rehearse all the times He opened doors, gave you promotions, healed your family members, and put you in the right places with the right people. Don't forget your victories. On a regular basis go back over your memorial stones, and read the victories etched on your staff.

When those negative memories come up, they come to all of us—the things that didn't work out, your hurts, your failures, and your disappointments. Many people mistakenly stay on that channel and they end up stuck in a negative rut and do not expect anything good. Remember, that's not the only channel—get your remote control and switch over to the victory channel.

Expect breakthroughs. Expect problems to turn around. Expect to rise to new levels. You haven't seen your greatest victories. You haven't accomplished your greatest dreams. There are new mountains to climb, new horizons to explore.

Don't let past disappointments steal your passion. Don't let the way somebody treated you sour you on life. God is still in control. It may not have happened in the past, but it can happen in the future.

Draw a line in the sand and say, "That's it. I'm done with low expectations. I'm not settling for mediocrity. I expect favor, increase, and promotion. I expect blessings to chase me down. I expect this year to be my best year so far."

If you raise your level of expectancy, God will take you places you've never dreamed. He'll open doors no man can shut. He will help you overcome obstacles that looked insurmountable, and you will see His goodness in amazing ways.

CHAPTER FOUR

Have a Positive Mind-set

Every day we get to choose our attitudes. We can determine to be happy and look on the bright side—expecting good things, and believing we will accomplish our dreams—or we can elect to be negative by focusing on our problems, dwelling on what didn't work out, and living worried and discouraged.

These are the choices we all can make. Nobody can force you to have a certain attitude. Life will go so much better if you simply decide to be positive. When you wake up, choose to be happy. That is the fourth undeniable quality of a winner.

Choose to be grateful for the day. Choose to look on the bright side. Choose to focus on the possibilities.

A good attitude does not automatically come. If you don't choose it, then more than likely you'll default to a negative mind-set, thinking: "I don't *Choose to be positive* feel like going to work. I've got so many obstacles. Nothing good is in my future."

A negative attitude will limit your life.

We all face difficulties. We all have tough times, but the right attitude is, "This is not permanent, it's only temporary. In the meantime I'm going to enjoy my life."

Maybe you didn't get the promotion you worked hard for, or you didn't qualify for that house you wanted. You could easily live with a sour attitude. Instead, you should think: "That's all right. I know something better is coming."

If you become caught in traffic, think positively: "I'm not going to be stressed. I know I'm at the right place at the right time."

If your medical report wasn't good, you can choose to think: "I'm not worried. This too shall pass."

If your dream is taking longer than you thought, you can choose to think: "I'm not discouraged. I know the right people, and the right opportunities are already in my future, and at the right time it will come to pass."

Set your mind to positive

When you have this positive mind-set, you cannot be defeated. No matter what comes your way, you shake it off and keep moving ahead.

Life is like a car; you have a forward gear and a reverse gear. You decide which way you want to go. It doesn't take any more effort to go forward than it does backward. If you choose to focus on the positive and keep your mind set on your possibilities, then you will move forward and see increase and favor.

But if you dwell on the negative and stay focused on problems and what you don't have, and how impossible your dream looks, that's just like putting your car in reverse—you'll go backward. It's all about what you choose to dwell on. You can choose to dwell on what's wrong with you or what's right with you. You can choose to look at how far you've got to go, or you can look at how far you've already come.

There is good and bad in every situation. If you'll have the right attitude, you can always find the good. It's like this little boy I heard about. He had a baseball bat and a ball and he said to himself, "I'm the best hitter in all the world."

He threw the ball up, swung, and missed: Strike one!

The boy picked up the ball, straightened his cap, and said it again: "I'm the best hitter in all the world."

He tossed the ball up and swung and missed again: Strike two!

This time he said it with even more determination: "I'm the best hitter in all the world!"

He tossed the ball up, swung away, and missed again. Strike three!

The boy then laid down the bat, smiled real big, and said, "What do you know? I'm the best *pitcher* in all the world."

Be like this boy and stay positive. That's a winner's mind-set. Learn to look on the bright side. Find the silver lining in every cloud.

A lot of people use the excuse, "I'm negative because I've had negative things happen to me." They'll offer excuses like these:

"My business didn't make it."

"A friend did me wrong."

"I had a bad childhood."

"I'm dealing with a sickness, and that's why I'm sour."

It's not your circumstances that make you negative, it's your attitude about those circumstances. You can take twenty positive people and twenty negative people and give them the exact same problem—put them on the same job, in the same family, and at the same house—and the twenty positive people will come out just as positive and happy, with great attitudes. The negative people will still be just as negative. They can have the same problems and same circumstances, but much different attitudes.

What's the difference? Positive people have made up their minds to enjoy life. They focus on the possibility, not the problem. They're grateful for what they have, and they don't complain about what they don't have. Positive people know that God is in control, and that nothing happens without His permission. They choose to bloom where they are planted. They're not waiting to be happy when the situation changes. They're happy while God is changing the situation.

When you're positive, you're passing the test. You're saying, "God, I trust you. I know you're fighting my battles."

If you are not happy where you are, you won't get where you want to be. Don't wait for everything to change before you have a good attitude. If you have a good attitude now, God can change the situation.

Keep the right perspective

Some people would love to have your problems. They would gladly trade places with you. They would love to have the job that frustrates you. They would love to sit in traffic in that car you don't like. They would love to have your husband, who gets on your nerves. They would love to live in the house you think is too small.

You may be thinking, "As soon as I get out of this neighborhood, then I'm going to be happy." Instead, why don't you choose to be happy right where you are? Choose to have a good attitude without thinking about what you have or don't have.

Your happiness is all about your approach to life. One man gets up and says, "Good morning, Lord." Another man gets up and says, "Oh Lord, it's morning." Which person are you?

You control what kind of day you're having. You're as happy as you want to be. It's not your circumstances that keep you unhappy. It's how you respond to them.

A lot of times we're making ourselves unhappy. You can't change the traffic, the weather, or how others treat you. If your happiness is based on everything going your way and everybody treating you right, you will be frustrated.

Before you leave the house, you need to make up your mind to stay positive and enjoy the day no matter what comes your way. You have to decide ahead of time.

That's what it says in Colossians 3:2, "Set your mind on the higher things and keep it set." The higher things are the

> Set your mind on
> higher things

positive things. When you get out of bed in the morning, you need to set your mind for victory. Set your mind for success.
Have the attitude: "This is going to be a great day. God's favor is on my life. I'm excited about my future."

When your mind is set as positive, hopeful, and expecting good things, that's when you'll go places you've never dreamed. New doors will open. New opportunities, and the right people will come across your path.

But if you don't set your mind, negative thoughts will set it for you. You can't start the day in neutral. If you're passive, lying in bed, negative thoughts like these will come: "You'll never accomplish your dreams. You'll never get married. You're too old. You'll never get well. Nothing good ever happens to you. You'll never get out of debt."

Set your mind for victory

You may not realize it, but that's setting the tone for defeat, for failure, for a lousy day. The first thing you should do is get your mind going in the right direction. This is why many people don't have enough energy, joy, vision, or passion. Their minds are set on the negative. It's been that way so long they don't know any better. It's normal to them.

They go through the day expecting problems, bad breaks, to barely get by, and to be mistreated. They live by Murphy's Law, which says, "If anything can go wrong, it will, and at the worst possible time. Things will take longer than you thought. It will be more difficult than it seems."

Because these people haven't set their minds, they expect negative things to happen. They wonder why they have such a tough time, and why they can't get ahead. It's because they're setting their minds for defeat, for bad breaks, for failure.

If you have fallen into that negative mind-set, you've got to change your outlook. You are a child of the most high God. You've been crowned with favor. You were never created to live an average, get-by, short-end-of-the-stick life. You were created to be the head and not the tail, to lend and not borrow, to reign in life as a king. You have royalty in your blood. Winning is in your DNA.

Now get rid of that negative mentality, and set your mind for victory. Set your mind for increase. Set your mind for good breaks. Start expecting your plans to work out. Expect people to be good to you. Expect to have a productive day.

If it doesn't happen, don't fall back into that old negative mentality by thinking things like: "I should have known it would not work out for me. I never get good breaks. I never find a good parking spot. These people never treat me right. It always takes me longer than anyone else."

You are not a victim. You're a victor. You wouldn't have opposition if there were not something amazing in your future. Keep a smile on your face. Keep a spring in your step. Stay positive. Stay hopeful. God is still on the throne.

Being sour, negative, and pessimistic, and expecting the worst, will keep you from your destiny. You may have had a lot of negative, unfair things happen in your past, but don't let that become a stronghold, or a mind-set where you think that's all there's ever going to be. Don't live with that negative mentality.

If God showed you all He has planned for you, it would boggle your mind. If you could see the doors He's going open, the opportunities that will cross your path, and the people who will show up, you'd be so amazed, excited, and passionate, it would be easy to set your mind for victory.

This is what faith is all about. You got to believe it before you see it. God's favor is surrounding you like a shield. Every setback is a setup for a comeback. Every bad break, every disappointment, and every person who does you wrong is part of the plan to get you to where you're supposed to be.

Don't fall into the trap of being negative, complacent, or just taking whatever life brings your way. Set the tone for victory, for success, for new levels. Enlarge your vision. Make room for God do something new. You haven't touched the surface of what He has in store.

Get your hopes up

I was talking to a reporter one time, and I could tell he didn't like the fact that my message is so positive and so hopeful. He asked what I would tell a person who lost a job and was about to lose a home and had no place to go and all sorts of other problems. He painted the worst possible situation.

I said, "First of all, I would encourage that person to get up and find something to be grateful for, and secondly, I would encourage the person to expect things to turn around, expect new doors to open, expect breakthroughs."

The scripture says, "When darkness overtakes the righteous, light will come bursting in." When you don't see a way out, and it's dark, you're in prime position for God's favor to come bursting in.

The reporter said, "Wouldn't that be giving them false hope?"

Here's the alternative: I could tell them be negative, bitter, give up, complain, and be depressed. All that would do is make matters worse.

You may be in a difficult situation, but instead of being negative just dig in your heels and say, "I refuse to live with a negative attitude. I'm not giving up on my dreams. I'm not living without passion or zeal. I may not see a way, but I know God has a way. It may be dark, but I'm expecting the light to come bursting in. I'm setting my mind for victory."

> *Let God's favor come bursting in*

That's what allows God to work. It's not just mind over matter. It's not just having a positive attitude. It's your faith being released. When you believe, it gets God's attention. When you expect your dreams to come to pass, your health restored, and good breaks and divine connections coming your way, then the Creator of the universe goes to work.

You may have had a thousand bad breaks, but don't use that as an excuse to be negative. One good break can make up for all the bad breaks. One touch of God's favor can catapult you further than you ever imagined. You may feel like you're getting behind. You're not where you thought you would be in life. Don't worry; God knows how to make up for lost time. He knows how accelerate things.

Now you've got to do your part. Shake off a negative mentality. Shake off pessimism, discouragement, and self-pity. Get your fire back. Life is passing you by. You don't have time to waste being negative. You have a destiny to fulfill. You have an assignment to accomplish. What's in your future is greater than anything you've seen in your past. We need to get rid of Murphy's Law and live by just the opposite. Your attitude should be: "If anything can go right today, it will go right and happen to me at the best time. Nothing will be as difficult as it looks. Nothing will take as long as it seems."

Why? You are highly favored. Almighty God is breathing in your direction. You've been anointed, equipped, and empowered.

Some may claim I'm just getting hopes up, and trying to get people to be more positive. It's true, and here's why: God is a positive God. There is nothing negative about Him. If you're negative, sour, or pessimistic, you're going against the flow of God.

When we fly from Houston to Los Angeles, it always takes thirty minutes longer to get there than it does to come home. It's because the jet stream flows from west to east. When we're headed there, there's a large mass of air always blowing against us, slowing us down. The other day we had a 120-mile-per-hour headwind. The plane has to work harder, use more fuel, and expend more energy.

But when we travel back home, it's just the opposite. The jet stream is working in our favor, pushing us forward and making it easier, saving us time and energy.

The same principles apply in life. When you are positive, hopeful, and expecting good things, you are in the jet stream of almighty God. Things will be easier. You will accomplish more, live happier, and see increase and favor. But when you are negative, discouraged, everything's a struggle; you have to work harder and you can't enjoy life.

Pay attention to what you're thinking about

You can't think negative thoughts and live a positive life. When you think, "I'll never pass this chemistry test. I dread going to work. My marriage will not last. I'll never meet the right person," that's going against the flow.

Your life follows your thoughts. You're drawing in what you're thinking about, just like a magnet.

"I can't pass this test."

You're drawing in defeat.

"I can't stand going to work."

You're drawing in negativity.

"I'll never meet the right person."

You're drawing in loneliness.

"I'll never accomplish my dreams."

You're drawing in mediocrity.

I read a study done on people who needed arthroscopic knee surgery. Their knees were worn down and they needed the joint to be cleaned out. On some of the patients, the doctors received family permission to only pretend to do the surgery as part of this study. Instead of actually cleaning out the knee and performing the full surgery, they simply put the patient under anesthesia and made three tiny incisions around the knee as if they had done something.

When those patients woke up, they thought their surgery had been performed. It's interesting that after two years, the patients who'd had the fake surgery reported just as much relief from the pain as the patients who'd actually had the surgery.

You may think that the patients who did not get the surgery were feeling no pain because their minds had been tricked. That wasn't the case. When the doctors examined their knees over time, they could see improvements, even without the surgery. Their conclusion was that when the brain expected the knee to get better, it did, even without surgery. Just thinking that the knee was healed actually helped the body to heal.

But how many people have programmed their mind to expect defeat, failure, and mediocrity? They've said a thousand times, "I'll never get well." Then their brains go to work according to that nega-tive thinking and send out this

> *Program your mind for success*

message: "Let's make sure he never gets well. Let's bring inflammation, sickness, and discomfort."

How many people go through the day feeling unquali-fied, inferior, and insecure? Their brains say, "I've got my instructions. Let me perform what they're asking. I've got to make sure they're clumsy and slow, and they don't have any good ideas. They make mistakes."

What's the problem? They have programmed themselves for defeat. Their minds are working just perfectly.

The good news is this also works in the right direction. When you go through the day saying, "I'm equipped, I'm empowered, and I am well able," your brain goes to work saying, "Let's make sure this person is at the top of the game, skilled, intelligent, creative, confident, and secure."

You may be facing a sickness, but you should not say, "I'll never get well." Instead, say, "I'm getting better and better.

Health and healing are flowing through me. God is renewing my youth."

The brain goes to work saying to your whole system: "Do you hear what she's saying? She says she's healthy. She's whole. She's strong. Get busy and release the healing. Create new cells. Unleash strength, energy, and vitality."

Maybe you struggle with an addiction. Don't ever say, "I'll never overcome it. I'm just hooked." If you believe you're an addict, then you'll always be an addict.

When you dwell on negative, defeated thoughts, you poison your system. You are telling your command center, your mind—this incredible tool God has given you—to release defeat, failure, and mediocrity. That's why the scripture says you have to guard your mind.

If you're trying to lose weight, don't ever say, "I'll never lose this weight. I'm so undisciplined. My metabolism is so messed up, even if I worked out all day it wouldn't make a difference."

When you do that your mind tells your system, "Stay messed up. Keep every calorie you can. Send out new cravings. Take away the desire to exercise. Make sure they feel bad, deplete all their energy."

When you get up in the morning, no matter how you feel, say to yourself, "I'm getting thinner. This weight is coming off. I'm strong, healthy, and energetic. I have discipline and self-control. I look good. I feel good. I think good."

Focus on the positive

Here's the key: Just because a thought comes doesn't mean you have to dwell on it. You control the doorway to your mind. If the thought is negative, discouraging, and pushing you down, then dismiss it. Don't dwell on it. Keep the door closed. Choose to dwell on thoughts that empower you, inspire you, and encourage you to have faith, hope, and joy.

If you keep your mind filled with the right thoughts, there won't be any room for the wrong thoughts. All through the day you should be focused on the positive: "Something good is going to happen to me. I'm strong, healthy, talented, disciplined. I'm fun to be around. My children will be mighty in the land. I can do all things through Christ. I will pass this chemistry test. I will meet the right person. I will overcome this challenge. My best days are still out in front of me."

When your mind is filled with thoughts of faith, hope, and victory, you will draw in the good things of God.

I read about a lady who had been sick for several years. She tried different doctors, but they couldn't figure out what was wrong. She was very negative, always talking about how she would never get well. Like a magnet, she kept drawing in more sickness.

The real battle takes place in your mind. What are you dwelling on all day? That's what you're attracting.

This lady went to another doctor and complained and told him she would never get well. Her negative comments went on and on. The doctor noticed her negative attitude. He decided to give her an unusual prescription. He'd never done this before.

The doctor said, "Every hour that you're awake, I want you to say at least six times, 'I'm getting better and better every day in every way.'" She thought that was strange and said, "Doctor, I'm not going to do that. I want some real medicine."

"No, you follow my orders, and then we'll talk about what's next," he said.

The patient started doing this fifty to sixty times a day, and before long her attitude began to change. Within a few days, she was feeling better. A couple of weeks later, her strength returned, and then her joy was back.

A month later, she was a different person. All the symptoms were gone. She went back to the doctor. He looked at the report on her blood work and said everything was perfectly normal.

What made the difference? She changed her thinking. Instead of drawing in sickness, she started drawing in health.

Sometimes your body will not get well until your mind tells it to get well. You won't accomplish your dreams by thinking, "I never get any good breaks. I don't know the right people. I don't have the funds or the education."

Give yourself permission to accomplish your dreams

You have to give yourself permission to accomplish your

dreams, permission to get out of debt, and permission to over-come the obstacle. Your better days begin in your thinking.

Studies show that when you are negative and think sad, discouraging thoughts, your serotonin level goes down, and that causes you to feel sad. It's not just in your head. It affects your moods. But when you get up each day in a positive frame of mind, feeling hopeful and expecting good things, endorphins are released that make you feel happy. You will have more energy, because being positive puts a spring in your step.

If you go around with negative thoughts, they will drain you of your faith, your energy, and your zeal. It's just like a big vacuum pulling out all the good things that God put in you. You'd be amazed at how much bet-ter you'd feel, how much more you'd accomplish, and how much further you'd go if you'd just switch over to this posi-tive mind-set.

You have to think positive thoughts on purpose. "This is going to be a great day. This is my year. I'm expecting an abundance of favor."

The scripture says, "Put on a fresh new attitude." I've found yesterday's attitude is not good enough for today. Every morning you have to consciously adopt a fresh atti-tude by thinking things like: "I'm going to be happy today. I'm going to be good to people. I'm going to go with the flow and not get upset. I know God is in control. He's directing my steps. No obstacle is too big. No dream is too great. I am well able to do what I'm called to do."

That fresh new attitude will put you in God's jet stream.

You will accomplish things that you could not accomplish on your own. You'll be more productive. You'll have more wisdom, creativity, and good ideas. You will overcome obstacles that were bigger, stronger, and more powerful.

Freshen up your attitude

A lot of people rely on yesterday's attitude, or last week's attitude, or last year's attitude. That thing is old and stale. Start putting on a fresh new attitude, every morning. Get your mind going in the right direction. Develop the habit of living in a positive mind-set.

This is what the Bible's Daniel did. The scripture says he had an excellent spirit. He was a cut above. He stood out in the crowd. How did he do it? Every morning he got up early, opened his window, and thanked God for the day. He thanked God for His goodness, and thanked Him that he was well able. He was putting on that fresh new attitude, setting his mind for victory.

Daniel was serving the king in a foreign land, when the king issued a decree that no one could pray to any God except the king's God. If they did, they would be thrown into a lion's den. That threat didn't stop Daniel. He got up every morning and kept praying to Jehovah.

Daniel's enemies told the king, who had already issued the decree. He loved Daniel, but he couldn't go back on his word. Daniel said, "Don't worry, King, I'm going to be fine. The God I serve is well able to deliver me."

That's what happens when you start the day off in faith, thinking positive thoughts on purpose. When you're in a difficult situation, you don't shrink back in fear with thoughts like: "Why is this happening to me?" Instead, you rise up in

Rise up in faith

faith and say, "My God is well able. I'm armed with strength for this battle. I can do all things through Christ. If God be for me, who dare be against me?"

The authorities threw Daniel into the lion's den with more than one hundred hungry lions. Everyone expected Daniel to be eaten in a few minutes. But when you have this attitude of faith, God will fight your battles for you.

God sent an angel to close the mouths of the lions. The king came by the next morning, and there was Daniel lying on the grass resting. The king got him out and said, "From now on we're going to all worship the God of Daniel, the true and living God."

It's interesting that the scripture says nothing negative about Joseph and Daniel. I'm sure they made mistakes, but you can't find a record of anything they did wrong. There are stories of other great heroes of faith like Abraham, David, Moses, Paul, and Peter failing and making mistakes.

Daniel and Joseph were good people, but they had bad circumstances. Unfair things happened to them. They were mistreated and faced huge obstacles. If you study their lives you'll find one common denominator: They were always positive. They had this attitude of faith. They didn't make excuses or say things like "God, why is this happening to me?"

They started off each day with their minds going in the right direction, knowing that our God is well able. They both saw favor and blessings in amazing ways. In the same way, you can be a good person and have bad circumstances.

It's easy to get negative and say things such as: "I don't understand why my child got off course. Why did I come down with this sickness? Why did these people do me wrong?"

Instead, do as Daniel did. Get up every morning in the midst of the battle, look up and say, "Lord, thank You for another great day. I know you are well able, bigger than my problem, greater than this sickness, and more powerful than my enemy. Thank You that today things will change in my favor."

Especially in difficult times, make sure you put on that fresh new attitude. Set your mind for victory and keep it set. When negative thoughts come, dismiss them and make a declaration like Daniel's: "My God is well able. He's done it for me in the past and I know He'll do it for me again in the future."

My challenge today is for you to keep your mind going in the right direction. When you're positive, you are in the jet stream of God. Learn to think thoughts on purpose: "This will be a great day. Something good is going to happen to me."

Start off your day in faith. If you develop this positive

mind-set you'll not only be happier, healthier, and stronger, but also, I believe and declare, you will accomplish more than you ever imagined. You will overcome obstacles that looked impossible, and you will become everything God has created you to be. You can, you will!

CHAPTER FIVE

Commit to Excellence

We live in a society in which mediocrity is the norm. Many people do as little as they can to get by. They don't take pride in their work or in who they are. If somebody is watching, they may perform one way, but when nobody is watching they'll cut corners and take the easy way out.

If you are not careful, you can be pulled into this same mentality where you think it's okay to show up late to work, to look less than your best, or to give less than your best. But God doesn't bless mediocrity. God blesses excellence. I have observed that the fifth undeniable quality of a winner is a commitment to excellence.

When you have a spirit of excellence, you do your best whether anyone is watching or not. You go the extra mile. You do more than you have to.

Other people may complain about their jobs. They may go around looking sloppy and cutting corners. Don't sink to that level. Everyone else may be slacking off at work, compromising in school, letting their lawns go, but here's the key: You are not everyone else. You are a cut above. You are called to excellence. God wants you to set the highest standard.

You should be the model employee for your company. Your boss and your supervisors should be able to say to the new hires, "Watch him. Learn from her. Pick up the same habits. Develop the same skills. This person is the cream of the crop, always on time, great attitude, doing more than what is required."

When you have an excellent spirit like that, you will not only see promotion and increase, but you are honoring God. Some people think, "Let me go to church to honor God. Let me read my Bible to honor God." And yes, that's true, but it honors God just as much to get to work on time. It honors God to be productive. It honors God to look good each day.

When you are excellent, your life gives praise to God.

Honor God in all you do

That's one of the best witnesses you can have. Some people will never go to church. They never listen to a sermon. They're not reading the Bible. Instead, they're reading your life. They're watching how you live. Now, don't be sloppy. When you leave the house, whether you're wearing shorts or a three-piece suit, make sure you look the best you possibly can. You're representing almighty God.

When you go to work, don't slack off, and don't give a halfhearted effort. Give it your all. Do your job to the best of your ability. You should be so full of excellence that other people want what you have.

When you're a person of excellence, you do more than necessary. You don't just meet the minimum requirements; you go the extra mile. That phrase comes from the Bible. Jesus said it in Matthew 5:41—"If a soldier demands you carry his gear one mile, carry it two miles." In those days Roman soldiers were permitted by law to require someone else to carry their armor.

Exceed expectations

Jesus said, "Do more than is expected; carry it two miles." That's the attitude you need to have: "I'm not doing just what I have to. I'm not doing the minimum amount to keep my job. I'm a person of excellence. I go above and beyond what's asked of me. I do more than is expected." This means if you're supposed to be at work at 8 a.m., you show up ten minutes early.

You produce more than you have to. You stay ten minutes late. You don't start shutting down thirty minutes before closing. You put in a full day. Many people show up to work fifteen minutes late. They get some coffee, wander around the office, and finally sit down to work a half hour late. They'll waste another half hour making personal phone calls and surfing the Internet. Then they wonder why they aren't promoted. It's because God doesn't reward sloppiness. God rewards excellence.

In the Old Testament, Abraham sent his servant to a foreign country to find a wife for his son, Isaac. Abraham told the servant that he would know he'd found the right lady if she offered a drink to both him and his camels. The servant reached the city around sunset. A beautiful young lady named Rebekah came out to the well. The servant said, "I'm so thirsty. Would you mind lowering your bucket and getting me a drink?"

She said, "Not only that, let me get some water for your camels as well."

Here's what's interesting: After a long day's walk, a camel can drink thirty gallons of water. This servant had ten camels with him. Think about what Rebekah did. If she had a one-gallon bucket of water, she said, in effect, "Yes I'll not only do what you asked and give you a drink, but I'll also dip down in this well three hundred more times and give your ten camels a drink."

Rebekah went way beyond the call of duty. As a result, she was chosen to marry Isaac, who came from the wealthiest family of that time. I doubt that she ever again had to draw three hundred gallons of water.

God rewards excellence. When you do more than what's required, you will see God's goodness in new ways.

You may be declaring favor and promotion over your life and that's all good, but it's only one part. The second part is making sure you get to work on time, do more than what's required, and do better this year than last year.

We're in a very competitive marketplace. If you're not growing, improving, and learning new skills, then you're falling behind.

On Sunday afternoons after our final service, I sit down

with a video editor and I edit my own sermons. I've done over 625 messages in fifteen years. Surely I don't need to watch another one. If I haven't gotten it down by now, it's never going to happen.

Still, I study each one to see what's good and what could be better. I'll see that one point took a little too long to develop, or that another section of the speech was really great. Maybe I'll see that I'm talking a little fast or that I need to look out at one side of the audience more.

I'm constantly evaluating and analyzing not only my speaking performance, but also the production, the lighting, and the camera angles. My attitude is that there's always room for improvement. We can always get better.

People watching on television will sometimes say, "Joel, I never hear you stutter, and I never hear you make a mistake." I always tell them it's because I know how to edit! I did that for seventeen years. I can fix every stutter, every pause. I don't have to. My live broadcasts aren't bad, but I want my taped sermons to be the best they can possibly be. I don't want to be at the same level next year as I am now. I want to be more effective, more skilled, and making a greater impact.

Strive for excellence

When you're an excellent person you don't get stagnant. You're always taking steps to improve. Favor and being excellent go hand in hand. Increase, promotion, and reaching your highest potential are all tied to a spirit of excellence.

Looking your best and taking care of your possessions are also part of this lifestyle. Some people—and I say this respectfully—drive cars that haven't been washed in six months. It used to be two-tone. Now it's four-tone. It would get better gas mileage if they washed it. They argue that it's an old piece of junk and that they're planning on getting a better car. But if you don't take care of what God has given you, how can He bless you with more?

I've been in huts in Africa with dirt floors and no running water, but they are spotless. Everything is clean, organized, perfectly in place. Why is that? The people who live there have a spirit of excellence. Whether you have much or a little, whether it's old or new, take pride in what God has given you.

After services in our church, I usually walk up to the visitor's area to greet our guests. On the way, if I see a piece of paper on the floor, a gum wrapper or a bulletin, I always pick it up. I don't have to do that. Somebody on our staff will get it eventually, but when you have this spirit of excellence, it's ingrained in you. To see any trash on the floor rubs me the wrong way.

Sometimes children from our nurseries drop crackers on the hallway floor. I always ask my assistant to call the cleaning crew if there is a big mess. I don't want people coming to the next service to see that on the floor. Why is that? It's not excellence if there is a mess on the floor. I realize our building represents almighty God. I have a responsibility to make sure it looks excellent. That's why we keep it painted. We make sure the lawn looks perfect, the hallways are spotless, the equipment works, the cameras are state-of-the-art, and the broadcast is exceptional.

Why? We represent God, and He is not sloppy. God is not run-down. God is not second-class. He is an excellent God.

It doesn't mean you must have the best to represent Him, but you should take care of what you have as best you can. Sometimes a can of paint can make all the difference in the world. Pulling some weeds, cleaning the carpet, getting more organized. Do what you can to represent God in an excellent way.

When our children were small we took them to Disneyland. That place was spotless. I never once saw gum stuck to the floor. Hundreds of thousands of people go through every year, and the entire park looked brand-new. I thought, "How do they do it?" One day, I saw employees going around with tools that scrape up gum. That's what they do all day long.

If Disney can keep their parks that clean and that first-class, we should make God's house clean and first-class. Now apply the same standards to your own life, your house, your car, your clothes, your cubicle, and your office. I'm not talking about spending a lot of money. It's how you choose to take care of what God's given you. I'm asking you to do it with excellence.

Do it with excellence

Years ago, I was driving to the church building we occupied prior to our current home. For some reason that day I noticed many in that area were not taking care of their homes. The yards weren't mowed. Weeds were everywhere. Things were stored all over the place.

Not to be critical, but it just looked sloppy, one house after another. As I continued driving, I noticed in the midst of all those houses there was this one house that stood out. The lawn was mowed. The yard was immaculate. The house was painted. Everything was perfectly in place.

When I got to church, I commented on that house and somebody said, "Don't you know that's So-and-So's house? They're some of our most faithful members." That didn't surprise me one bit. Lakewood people are people of excellence.

They stood out in the crowd. They were a cut above. They easily could have had the attitude, "Nobody else takes care of their homes, why should we?" But they chose to have an excellent spirit.

You may be in a situation today in which everybody around you is being lazy. Everybody's being sloppy. Everybody's taking the easy way out. Don't let that rub off on you. You should be the one to have an excellent spirit. You should be the one to stand out in the crowd.

You may say, "Joel, you mean I bought this book so you would tell me to clean up my house?" Not just that, you should mow the lawn, too! And organize the garage while you're at it.

Seriously, what kind of example is it to your friends, your neighbors, and your coworkers if your yard is sloppy and your car is never washed and you show up late to work? That's not a good representation, and the truth is that's not who you are. God made you as a person of excellence. Maybe all you've seen modeled is mediocrity, or sloppiness—and maybe the people you work around are always late and undisciplined. But God is calling you to set a new standard.

He wants to take you places higher than you've ever dreamed of, but you've got to do your part and stir up the excellence on the inside. Don't make excuses. Don't say, "This is the way I've always been." Take this challenge and come up to a higher level of excellence.

This applies also to your personal appearance: the way you dress and the way you present yourself. We all have different styles and different tastes. There is no right and wrong. You may not like to wear a suit, and there is nothing wrong with that. The main thing is to present yourself in a way that you're proud of.

Don't go out feeling sloppy, feeling less than your best, or knowing that you didn't take the time to look like you should. You are the temple of the most high God.

Take care of yourself

God lives in you. Take time to take care of yourself. Some women, in particular, take care of everyone else, putting their children first, being good wives, and running the house or doing their jobs. That's good, but they need to take care of themselves, too.

Get your nails done. Get your hair done. Get a massage. Go shopping. Go exercise. Go have some fun with your friends. Take care of your temple in an excellent way.

Some men haven't bought new clothes in twenty-seven

years. The shirts they are wearing have been in and out of style three times already. They are taking care of their families. They are hard workers. Now they need to take care of themselves, too. When you look good you feel better.

One time Victoria asked me to run to the grocery store and pick up something so she could finish making dinner. I had just worked out. I was hot and sweaty and I was wearing this old, torn-up T-shirt and these run-down gym shorts that I used to wear all the time. My hair wasn't combed. I looked really bad, but I didn't feel like getting all cleaned up.

I just jumped in the car and headed up there, hoping I wouldn't see anyone. I pulled into the parking lot and I heard God speak to me—not out loud, just an impression down inside—"Joel, don't you dare go in there like that. Don't you realize you are representing me? I am the king of kings. I deserve respect and honor."

I turned around and drove all the way back home, took a shower, combed my hair, put on some clean clothes and went back and picked up those *TV dinners*! Just kidding! We have to understand that we represent almighty God. God does not like sloppiness. Even around the home, we all like to be super casual, but make sure you look good for your children and for your spouse.

Some ladies may need to get rid of bathrobes given to them by their great-grandmothers and buy something new. You may love them because they are comfortable and sentimental, but can I tell you what nobody else will tell you: They are ugly. You're too beautiful to wear those things. Get your credit cards and go to a certain store at the mall. I'm not going to give away a free advertisement, but it starts with my wife's name: Victoria. I can't tell you the whole thing because it's a *secret*. You can figure it out. Go get something that makes you look like the masterpiece God made you to be.

Make a habit of excellence

When you go to a store and you accidentally knock some clothes off the rack, don't leave them down there and act like you don't see them. A person of excellence picks them up and puts them back. When you're shopping for groceries and you decide you don't want the box of cereal any more, don't just stick it back over by the potato chips. A person of excellence takes the cereal box back where it was found.

Well, you say, "That's what those employees are paid to do." You should do it unto God. You should do it because you have an excellent spirit. A person of excellence doesn't park in the handicap spot because it's closer to the mall entrance. A person of excellence turns off the lights in the hotel room when leaving to save energy and costs for the hotel. They don't say, "Well, I'm paying good money for that room. I don't have to do that."

People of excellence go the extra mile to do what's right. They do that not because somebody is watching, and not because somebody is making them. They do it to honor God.

At our house we used to have these big five-gallon containers

Go the extra mile

of water. They were large glass bottles, and each with a neck, and you had upend them and put them on this special dispenser, and that's how you would get the water out. They were not only very heavy, but also very awkward. Victoria likes everything super clean. Even though the part where the water goes in was completely sealed, the receptor comes way up inside the bottle's neck. There's no way you can even get to it. You have to break the seal.

But Victoria insisted that the whole bottle get wiped down with soap. When that glass had soap on it, it would get very slippery, even after we dried it. I debated with her several times, saying that it wasn't necessary to wipe down the whole bottle. I was very passionate, but I couldn't convince her.

I gave her my word that I would do it. But there were plenty of times I was in the pantry all by myself, where nobody could see me, and I would start to put that bottle up without cleaning it, and I would hear that still small voice saying, "Joel, do the right thing. Be a person of excellence. Keep your word."

More than once, I've had it on the stand and I had to take it down and go get the soap. Excellence is doing the right thing even when nobody can see you. Even when you don't think it's necessary. Even when you don't agree. You gave your word, so you live up to it.

Sometimes you have to say, "God, I don't feel like doing this, but I will do it unto You. Or, I think my boss is unfair in telling me to do this, but I will do it unto You. Or, somebody else made the mess and I shouldn't have to clean it up, but God, I will do it unto You."

Pass the small test

Many people do not enjoy God's favor like they should, because they don't pass the small tests. Being excellent may not be some huge adjustment you need to make. It may mean just leaving ten minutes earlier so you can get to work on time. It may mean not complaining when you have to clean up. It may mean not making personal phone calls on work time—just a small thing. Nobody would know it. But the scripture says, "It's the little foxes that spoil the vines."

If I had put up that water bottle week after week without cleaning it, nobody would have known except God and me. I could have gotten away with it, but here's the key: I don't want something small to keep God from releasing something big into my life.

A while back, I was in a store's parking lot, and it was very windy outside. When I opened my car door, several pieces of trash blew out on the ground. As I went to pick them up, the wind caught them and they flew about fifteen or twenty feet in different directions. I didn't feel like going over to pick up those scraps. I looked around and there were already all kinds of other trash in the parking lot.

I was in a hurry. I came up with several good excuses why I shouldn't go pick them up. I almost convinced myself to let them go, but at the last moment I decided I was going to be a person of excellence and pick up my trash. The scraps had blown here and there. I ended up running all over that parking lot.

My mind was saying, "What in the world am I doing out here? It doesn't matter—let the stuff go." When I finally l picked up all of the scattered trash, I came back to my car. I had not realized it, but this couple was sitting in the car next to mine, watching the whole thing. They rolled the window down and said, "Hey, Joel. We watch you on television each week."

Then the lady said something very interesting. "We were watching to see what you were going to do."

I thought, "Oh, thank you, Jesus."

Whether you realize it or not, people are watching you. Make sure you're representing God the right way.

Distinguish yourself

I mentioned Daniel in the previous chapter. The scripture says he had an excellent spirit. As a teenager, he was brought out of Judah into Babylon. The king had all these young men in training and the best of them—the smartest, strongest, and most talented—would be chosen as the next leaders.

They had a certain diet for them to eat and certain programs for them to follow. But Daniel had made a vow to God to always honor Him. The Babylonians worshiped idols. Daniel was respectful, but he wouldn't eat the king's fancy foods. He didn't just go along with what everyone else was doing. He made the more excellent choice.

Daniel 6:3 says, "Daniel so distinguished himself by his exceptional qualities that the king planned to put him over the whole kingdom." Notice it doesn't say: "God distinguished him and he got promoted." It says Daniel distinguished himself. The message translation says, "Daniel completely outclassed the others."

That's what happens when, number one, you honor God and, number two, you have an excellent spirit. You don't compromise. You don't just go with the flow and do what everyone else is doing.

Even if everyone else is late, everyone else cuts corners, and everyone else is undisciplined, you should do as Daniel did and go the extra mile. Make the choice to be excellent.

Make the choice to be excellent

The scripture goes on to say Daniel was ten times smarter than the other young men. He had incredible wisdom and understanding. He could interpret dreams and visions. When you have an excellent spirit, God will give you unprecedented favor, creativity, and ideas so that, like Daniel, you will stand out in the crowd. In humility, you will outclass those who don't honor God.

My question is: Are you distinguishing yourself and not waiting for God to do it? Are you going the extra mile? Are you doing more than you have to? Are you improving your skills?

Examine your life. We all have areas in which we can

strive for excellence, whether it's how we treat people, how we present ourselves, or how we develop our skills. Don't let something small keep you from the big things God wants to do. You are called to be a cut above. You have excellence on the inside. It's who you are. Now do your part and be disciplined to bring out your excellence.

If you'll have this spirit of excellence, God will breathe in your direction and cause you to stand out. You'll look up and be more creative, more skilled, more talented, and wiser with more ideas. I believe and declare that like Daniel, you will outperform, you will outclass, and you will outshine, and God will promote you and set you in a place of honor. You can, you will.

CHAPTER SIX

Keep Growing

Too many people suffer from destination disease. They reach a certain level, earn their degrees, buy their dream homes, and then just coast.

Studies show 50 percent of high school graduates never read another entire book. One reason may be that they see learning as something you do in school, just something you do for a period of life instead of as a way of life.

We all learned when we were in school. Our teachers, coaches, and parents taught us. We were expected to learn when we were school age. But some tend to think that once they finish a certain level of education: "I'm done with school. I've finished my training. I've got a good job."

Winners never stop learning, and this is the sixth undeniable quality I have observed. God did not create us to reach one level and then stop. Whether you're

Never stop learning

nine or ninety years old, you should constantly be learning, improving your skills, and getting better at what you do.

You have to take responsibility for your own growth. Growth is not automatic. What steps are you taking to improve? Are you reading books or listening to educational videos or audios? Are you taking any courses on the Internet or going to seminars? Do you have mentors? Are you gleaning information from people who know more than you?

Winners don't coast through life relying on what they have already learned. You have treasure on the inside—gifts, talents, and potential—put in you by the Creator of the universe. But those gifts will not automatically come out. They must be developed.

I read that the wealthiest places on earth are not the oil fields of the Middle East or the diamond mines of South Africa. The wealthiest places are the cemeteries. Buried in the ground are businesses that were never formed, books that were never written, songs that were never sung, dreams that never came to life, potential that was never released.

Grow your gifts

Don't go to your grave with that buried treasure. Keep growing. Keep learning. Every day we should have a goal to grow in some way, to learn something new. Pablo Casals was one of the greatest cellists of all time. He started playing at the age of twelve and he accomplished things that no other cellist did. He was known around the world as the greatest in his field.

Yet, at the age of eighty-five, Casals still practiced five hours a day. A reporter asked him why he still put so much effort into it. He smiled and said, "I think I'm getting better."

Casals understood this principle: When you stop learning, you stop growing. Whatever you do, get better at it. Sharpen your skills. Don't be at the same level next year as you are right now. Like the great cellist, get better.

There are all kinds of opportunities to increase. There is more knowledge available today than any time in history. You have no excuse for not improving. You don't have to go to the library. You don't even have to travel to a university. With the Internet, information flows right into your home. The Internet wasn't created just to share pictures, play games, or look up movie times. That's all fine, but the Internet is a tool that can help you increase your gifts.

You have a responsibility not only to God, not only to your family, but also to yourself to develop what He's put in you. If you're in sales, human resources, auto mechanics, or health care, you can always expand your knowledge and improve your skills. Read books to learn how to communicate, work as a team member, or lead more effectively.

No matter what you do, there are people who have gone where you're going. Listen to what they have to say. Take twenty minutes a day, turn off the TV, and invest in yourself.

You should be doing something intentional and strategic every day to improve your skills. Don't be vague in your approach. Do not say things such as: "If I have time, I'll do it."

You are better than that. You've got too much in you to stay where you are. Your destiny is too great to get stuck.

A lot of times we sit back and think, "God, I'm waiting on you, I'm waiting for that big break." Let me tell you who gets the big breaks—people who are prepared, those who develop their skills continuously.

You've got to be proactive to take these steps to grow. When God sees you doing your part and developing what He's given you, then He'll do His part and open up doors that no man can shut. You may be tempted to say, "Well, Joel, I'm so busy. I don't have time to take any training courses. I don't have time to read books, learn new things. I'll get behind."

That's the wrong attitude. It's like these two lumberjacks who were out chopping down trees. One said, "I'm going to take a break and go sharpen my axe." The other said, "I don't have time to stop. I've got too much work to do. Sharpening my axe will put me behind."

He kept chopping and chopping. The other man went out and sharpened his axe. He came back three hours later, chopped down twice as many trees as his friend with the dull axe. Sometimes you need to take a break and sharpen your axe. If you sharpen your skills you won't need to work as hard. If you sharpen your skills, you'll get more done in less time. You will be more productive.

Don't settle

Whether you are a teacher, a carpenter, a banker, or a doctor, don't settle where you are. Don't coast or rest on your laurels. Stir up what God has put in you and get better at it. Sharpen your axe.

> *Don't coast or rest on your laurels*

This is a call to action. There are new levels in your future. Things have shifted in your favor. God is looking for people who are prepared and taking steps to improve. He is looking for those who are serious about fulfilling their destinies.

Think about David in the Bible. He was out in the shepherd fields taking care of his father's sheep. In today's terms he had a boring minimum wage job and no friends, and it didn't look like there was any opportunity for growth.

David's brothers got the good jobs. They were in the army. That was prestigious. They were admired and respected.

David could have slacked off, been sloppy, unmotivated, and thought, "No reason to develop my skills, I have no opportunity, I'm stuck out here with these sheep."

Instead, while he was alone, he did not sit around bored and waste time. He practiced using his slingshot day after day and month after month. I can envision him setting up a target, slinging rocks again and again, learning, getting better, making adjustments, and sharpening his skills.

When a coyote or wild animal came after his sheep, no

problem for David. He would get that slingshot out and nail it. He was like a sharpshooter, a marksman, so precise, so skillful; he could hit a bull's-eye from a hundred meters away.

When God sought somebody to defeat a giant, somebody to lead His chosen people, He looked to see who was prepared. He wanted someone who had developed their skills, who had taken the time to cultivate the gifts He had put in them. He didn't choose just anybody—He selected a skilled marksman who could hit a target with precision.

In the same way, when God seeks somebody to promote, He doesn't just randomly close His eyes and say, "I'll pick this one. You won the lottery. It's your lucky day."

No, God looks for people who have developed their skills. When we read about David standing before Goliath and slinging that rock, sometimes we think it was all God's hand at work. In a sense it was God, but the truth is God didn't sling the rock. God didn't cause the rock to hit Goliath in just the right place.

It was David, who developed and used the skills God gave him. Like David, God has put in you a set of special skills that will slay giant challenges, and open new doors—skills that will thrust you to new levels.

But here's the key: Your skills have to be developed. Every day you spend learning, growing, and improving will prepare you for that new level.

Prepare yourself to be a winner

You may be in a lower-position job, doing something that seems insignificant. But you know you have so much more in you. It would be easy to slack off and think, "There's no future here. I'll prepare as soon as I get out of this place, when good breaks come my way, or when the boss promotes me. Maybe then I'll take some courses, lose a few pounds, have a better attitude, and buy some nicer clothes."

That's backward. You must start improving right where you are. Start sharpening your skills while you're waiting. Study your manager's work habits. Study your best supervisor. Learn how to do their jobs. Be ready to step into those shoes.

When God sees you prepare yourself, then He opens new doors. The scripture says, "A man's gifts makes room for him." If no new doors are opening, don't be discouraged. Just develop your gifts in a new way. Improve your skills.

You might feel that your supervisors aren't going anywhere right now, but if you outgrow them, outperform them, out produce them, and know more than them, your gifts will make room for you. Somewhere, somehow, and some way God will open a door and get you where He wants you to be.

Don't worry about who is ahead of you or when your time will come. Just keep growing, learning, and preparing. When you are ready, the right doors will open.

The fact is God may not want you to have your supervisor's position. That may be too low for you. He may want to thrust you right past your boss and put you at a whole new level. I know former receptionists who went from answering the phones to running multi-million-dollar companies.

You can. You will. Develop what's in you, and you'll go farther than you can imagine.

Have you come down with destination disease? You're comfortable, not learning anything new. There's nothing wrong with that, but you have so much more in you.

You were created to increase

Studies tell us that the average person only uses 11 percent of the brain. Think of all that potential you could be tapping into. Maybe you're an accountant. That's good, but don't settle there. Why not get your CPA certification? That is a new skill you can develop. That gift will make more room for you.

Maybe you're an electrician, a plumber, or a mechanic. That's great, but what steps are you taking to improve your skills and your position in life? If you spend two hours a day improving on the same skills, in three years you will be an expert in that area.

Find what you're good at and keep improving on it. In today's competitive marketplace, with the economy so tight and business so bottom-line

Keep improving

oriented, if you're not improving then you're falling behind. If your skill levels are at the same place today they were five years ago, you're at a disadvantage.

I want to light a new fire under you. Shake off that destination disease. Sharpen your skills. I read an article about reducing the risk of being laid off. There were three main things that employers look for in determining who stays. They look for those with positive attitudes, flexibility, and the desire to keep learning and improving.

To be a winner, you need to develop your gifts to the point where your company can't make it without you. Or at least, you want your bosses to know things don't run nearly as smoothly when you're gone.

If you're out for a week and nobody misses you—sales are just as good, all the work gets done—that's okay as long as you own the company, but if you're an employee, that's alarming. If you're not being missed, then maybe you're not needed.

You need to kick it into a new gear. Produce more than you've been producing. Take some classes to increase your skills. Step it up a notch. Don't settle for a low position where no one will miss you. You have treasure in you. There is talent and skill that will cause you to be noticed. Proverbs 22:29 says, "Do you see a person skilled in their work? They will stand before kings and great men." Keep sharpening your skills. Cream always rises to the top.

This is what Joseph did in the Bible. He started off at the very bottom. He was thrown into a pit and sold into slavery by his brothers. Joseph didn't wait for vindication.

He decided to be his best. Even as a slave, he developed his gifts.

Joseph made himself so valuable that he was put in charge of his master's house. When he was falsely accused and put in prison, he was so organized, so wise, so skillful that they put him in charge of the whole prison.

Joseph was cream rising to the top. When Pharaoh needed someone to run the country, and administer the nationwide food program, Pharaoh didn't choose one of his own people. He didn't choose his department head, or a cabinet member. He chose Joseph, a prisoner, and a foreigner.

Why? Joseph developed his skills right where he was, and his gifts made room for him. Don't use where you are as an excuse to not grow. Don't say, "I'm not in a good job. I don't like my position. I've had unfair things happen. That's why I've lost my passion."

Remember, the treasure is still in you. God is saying it's time to use your gifts. Stretch yourself. Take some courses. Sharpen your skills. You should be so productive, so filled with wisdom no matter where you are, like Joseph, you will rise to the top.

Be the solution, not the problem

One way you'll be invaluable is learn to be a problem solver. That's what Joseph was. He was solution oriented. Don't go to your boss and say, "Our department is falling apart. This manager is about to quit. Bob cursed out Jim, and Bill keeps leaving early. Nobody paid our taxes last month. What do you want me to do?"

That's not the way to get promoted. If you present a problem, always present a solution as well. If you can't present a solution, hold it until you can figure out something.

A child can come tell me the building is on fire. That's easy. That doesn't take any skill. But I want somebody to tell me not only is the building on fire, but also the fire department is on the way, all the people are safe, the insurance company has been notified, and temporary quarters have been arranged. If you want to be invaluable to your organization, present your bosses with solutions, not problems.

What steps are you taking to better yourself so you can go to the next level? Are you reading books and trade magazines to stay up-to-date? Can you take a course to gain an advantage?

Develop the treasure within you

You've got to be on the offensive, even if you have your degree. Do you know many degrees are outdated in as little as five years? The world is changing so fast. If you don't continue learning and keep growing, you will fall behind.

I was talking to an airline pilot recently. He said pilots must go every year to update their training so they can continue flying. Why? The technology changes so fast.

Don't come down with destination disease. Break out of that box and learn something new. Will Rogers said, "Even if you're on the right track, if you just sit there, eventually you're going to get run over." If you don't take steps to keep growing, then don't be surprised if someone comes along and takes the promotion that belongs to you.

God has new levels in your future, but if you're not prepared for them—if you haven't developed the treasure He's put in you—then you can miss out on the fullness of what He has in store.

Every one of us should have a personal growth plan. Not something vague: "I'll read a book every once in a while. I'll take the company training this year." No, you need a specific plan that lays out how you're going to grow. It should include the steps you will take to get better.

Let me give you some ideas. Instead of listening to the radio driving to work, listen to good teaching audiobooks and CDs. Listen to training materials, and to other helpful material that will help you grow and improve in your field.

The average American spends three hundred hours a year in a car. You can turn your car into a university. That's valuable time. Imagine what you can learn in three hundred hours. Take advantage of it.

You can also listen to inspiring and informative audios while working out. I have people tell me all the time, "Joel, I listen to you while I run. I listen to you at the gym." One lady said, "I listen to you every night before I go to bed. You always put me right to sleep."

I thought, "Thanks a lot!"

Winners do the little things that count

These are simple things winners do to keep growing and bettering themselves. You don't have to spend three hours a day studying. Just take advantage of the time you're not using right now.

Podcasts are another great tool. You can download messages and listen to them whenever you want. This year we will give away 100 million copies of my messages at no charge. You can sign up for them on iTunes and listen as often as you want. That's a growth plan.

If you want to keep growing you need to have good mentors, people who have been where you want to go, people who know more than you. Let them speak into your life. Listen to their ideas. Learn from their mistakes. Study how they think and how they got to where they are.

I heard about a company that held a sales class for several hundred employees. The speaker asked if anyone knew the names of the top three salespeople. Every person raised a hand.

He then asked how many of them had gone to lunch with these top salespeople and taken time to find out how they do what they do? Not one hand went up.

There are people all around us whom God put in our paths on purpose so we can gain wisdom, insight, and experience, but we have to be open to learning from them. Look around and find the winners you could learn from.

I say this respectfully: Don't waste your valuable time with people who aren't contributing to your growth. Life is too short to hang around people who are not going anywhere. Destination disease is contagious. If you're with them long enough, their lack of ambition and energy will rub off on you.

Winners need to associate with inspiring people who build you up, people who challenge you to go higher, not anyone who pulls you down and convinces you to settle where you are. Your destiny is too important for that.

Young people often get caught up in trying to be popular instead of trying to be their best. I've found that in twenty years nobody will care whether you were popular in high school. Those who need attention and act up or wear a lot of bling and don't study because it isn't cool will find things change after high school.

Build a foundation for continuous growth

What matters, then, is having a good education, good work habits, and a good attitude that gives you a foundation to build on. Popularity is about wanting people to like you, but happiness is about liking yourself.

In most schools, the science fair is not the most popular event. Being in the math club isn't nearly as cool as being on the football team. Some of my friends made fun of people on the debate team. But now they work for people who were on the debate team.

Junior high and high school are critical times in our lives and our formative years. There's so much emphasis on sports and not enough on studies. I love sports. I played sports

> *Associate with inspiring people*

growing up, still do. They teach discipline and teamwork and perseverance, and that's all great. But we need to keep sports in perspective.

Most of us are not going to play sports for a living. One in one million kids will play professional basketball. I don't mean to depress you, but if you're white it's one in five million! The average professional football career is three and a half years. Even if you do make it, you still need a good foundation for life after football.

When you study and learn, and take school seriously you may be called a bookworm, a geek, or a nerd, but don't worry about those names. In a few years you'll be called the boss. You'll be called CEO, president, senator, pastor, or doctor.

Thomas Edison, Henry Ford, and Harvey Firestone had summer homes next to each other in Florida. They were close friends and spent much of their summers together.

Who you associate with makes a difference in how far you go in life. If your friends are Larry, Curly, and Moe, you may have fun, but you may not be going anywhere. The scripture says, "We should redeem the time." You need to see time as a gift. God has given us 86,400 seconds each today.

You're not being responsible with what God gave you if you're hanging out with time wasters who have no goals and no dreams.

You spend time just like you spend money

You have a destiny to fulfill. God has amazing things in your future. It's critical that you surround yourself with the right people. If you're the smartest one in your group, then your group is too small. You need to be around people who know more than you and have more talent than you. Don't be intimidated by them; be inspired.

If you take an oak tree seed and plant it in a five-gallon pot, that tree will never grow to the size it was created to be. Why? It's restricted by the size of the pot. In the same way, God has created you to do great things. He's put talent, ability, and skills on the inside. You don't want to be restricted by your environment. It may be too small.

Some of you are being restricted by your environment. It's too small. The people you hang around are negative and drag you down. You need to get out of that little pot. God created you to soar. It's fine to help people in need, but don't spend all your time with them.

You need talented and smart people in your life; winners who are farther along than you and can inspire you and challenge you to rise higher.

My question for you is this: Are you doing anything strategic and intentional to keep growing? If not, you can start right now. Come up with a personal growth plan. It can be something like, "I will get up every morning and spend the first twenty minutes meditating on the scripture. I will listen to a teaching CD driving to work. I will read a book fifteen minutes every night before I go to bed. I will meet with my mentor twice a month. I will be in church every weekend."

That's a definite plan. When you take responsibility for your growth, God will honor your efforts.

Promotion, good breaks, businesses, books, and divine connections are in your future. But now is the time to prepare. Don't get caught with destination disease.

There is treasure in you, waiting to be developed. Redeem the time. Make a decision to grow in some way every day. If you keep sharpening your skills, and getting better, God promises your gifts will make room for you.

Like David, because you are prepared, I believe and declare God is about to thrust you into the fullness of your destiny. He will open doors that no man can shut. You will go further than you could imagine and become the winner He's created you to be.

CHAPTER SEVEN

Serve Others

Jesus said if you want to be great in the kingdom, if you want to live a blessed life, there's a simple key: You have to serve other people. He wasn't talking about an event that happens every once in a while. He was talking about a life-style in which you live to help others, and you're always look-ing for ways to serve.

When you live a "serve others" lifestyle, you help friends, volunteer in your community, and take care of loved ones. It's not something you have to force yourself to do. It becomes a part of who you are. You develop an attitude of giving to everyone you meet. That's when you'll have true happiness and true fulfillment. You live not to receive, but to give.

Many people are not happy, because they are focused only on themselves. It's all about "my dreams, my goals, and my problems." That self-centered focus will limit you. You have to get your mind off of yourself.

You were created to give. God has put people in your life

on purpose so you can be a blessing to them. Every morning you should ask, "God, what is my assignment today? Help me to see the people you want me to be good to."

I've known my friend Johnny my whole life, more than forty years. He is constantly serving others. He's always

| Live to serve others |

running somebody to the airport, taking a friend to dinner, encouraging a pastor, or helping somebody on a project. When my father was on dialysis, if one of the family members couldn't take him to the clinic, we'd ask Johnny and he'd gladly do it.

I called Johnny one hot Saturday afternoon. When he picked up the phone, it was very noisy in the background. I could tell a lot was going on. I asked him where he was. He said, "I'm on top of a house. My friend's next door neighbor is an elderly lady, and we told her we'd reroof her house this weekend."

He didn't even know the lady. She was just the neighbor of a friend. But Johnny has developed this mentality to serve others. When you serve others, you are serving God. When you do it for them, you're doing it for Him.

Jesus said, "If you give a cup of cold water to someone in need, you will surely be rewarded." Every time you serve, God sees it. Every time you help someone else. Every time you sacrifice—you go out of your way to pick up a friend, you get up early to sing in the choir, you stay late to help a coworker—God is keeping the record.

Your reward is coming

Don't look for people to pay you back. They may not thank you. You may not get the credit. There may be no applause, but let me assure you, when you serve others there is applause in heaven. God sees your sacrifices.

You don't need people's applause. You don't need anyone cheering you on. You don't need the Employee of the Month plaque; you are doing it unto God. He's the One who matters. He sees your acts of kindness. He sees you volunteer at the hospital. He sees you show up each week to serve in the church nursery. He sees you taking your neighbor to the doctor on your day off. When you serve others, God says you'll be great in the kingdom.

J. J. Moses was a star football player in college. He was drafted by the Houston Texans and played for them for six years. He was the kick returner and punt returner. He was as fast as lightning! When he had the ball, he electrified fans, darting here and there. He was amazing to watch.

Playing in the National Football League in front of millions of fans, J.J. was at the pinnacle of success. But during the off seasons—and any time he didn't have a game—do you know where J.J. was every Saturday night?

J.J. was not at home with his feet up. He was not out enjoying his celebrity. He was at our church in Houston, serving others as an usher, helping people to their seats, showing visitors around, passing the offering plates, and making everyone feel welcome.

Many of those who came to church didn't know he was a star football player. In the stadium all the lights were on him. Fans wanted his autograph or pictures with him. J.J. could have allowed his fame to go to his head and thought, "I'm big-time, I'm not serving as an usher. I'm not waiting on people—I want them to wait on me."

Instead, J.J. told me, "My greatest honor was not playing in front of eighty thousand people in the stadium each week. My greatest honor was ushering in my section at Lakewood every Saturday night."

J.J. offers testimony to the fact that you are never too big to serve, never too important, never too influential. I knew another good man whose wealth was estimated at more than nine billion dollars. He's

You are never too big to serve

in heaven now, but he'd made it big in the oil business after starting with nothing. He loved God and always helped others. Among many other things, he owned a big retreat center where people could come and get away for a weekend and be refreshed.

One time a couple showed up at the retreat's front desk when the receptionist had stepped away. My friend the multibillionaire just happened to be there. He was an older man, very friendly and humble. He checked in the couple, gave them their keys, then grabbed their suitcases and carried them to the room. He set them up, laid out their bags, and even brought ice for them.

He was about to leave them when the lady pulled a

five-dollar bill from her purse and gave him a tip. She thought he was the bellman.

He just smiled and said, "Thank you, Lord, now I've got nine billion and five dollars!"

I love the fact that he wasn't too important to serve. He didn't say, "Excuse me, I don't need a tip. I own it all. Do you know who I am?"

It takes a big person to do something small. It takes humility to say, "I don't have to do this. It's not required of me. I could have somebody else do it. Nobody would fault me if I didn't, but I know in order to serve God, I need to serve other people."

If you want a great life, it doesn't just come from success, having a bigger house, or more accomplishments. There's nothing wrong with those things. God wants you to be blessed. But if you want to truly be fulfilled, you have to develop the habit of serving others.

You were created to give. You were created to make the lives of others better. Someone needs what you have. Someone needs your love. Someone needs your smile. Someone needs your encouragement and your gifts.

When you serve others, there will be a satisfaction that money can't buy. You'll feel a peace, a joy, a strength, and a fulfillment that only God can give. The Bible tells a story about Jesus and the disciples traveling a long way to Samaria. They were tired and hungry. Jesus sent the disciples into town to get food while He waited at the well. There He met a woman. He told her about her future and gave her a new beginning.

The disciples came back a few hours later with the food, but Jesus wasn't hungry anymore. He wasn't tired, either. He was sitting by the well satisfied, at peace. They were surprised. They tried to offer Him something to eat, but He wouldn't take it.

He said, "I have food that you know nothing about." They thought maybe somebody came while they were gone and gave Him something to eat. They talked about it: "He was tired a minute ago; now He's refreshed. He was hungry, but now He says He's satisfied. How could that be?"

Jesus overheard them trying to figure it out. He told them the secret. He said, "My meat is to do the will of Him that sent me, to accomplish his work." He was saying, "I get fed by doing what God wants me to do. I get nourished when I help people. My food, strength, peace, joy, and satisfaction come when I serve others."

Feed your soul through service

Sometimes you can work all day and you'll get tired physically. But there are times when you go out of your way to be a blessing. You get up early to help a coworker. You stop by the hospital and pray for a friend. You mow a neighbor's lawn after work.

Doing all that should make you tired and run-down, but you feel energized, stronger, and refreshed. Why is that?

When you do the will of your Father it doesn't drain you, it replenishes you. You may volunteer in your community each week. You may get up early and go to church on your day off, maybe serving in the children's ministry after working all week. You may clean houses in the community outreach Saturday morning. You may spend the afternoon at the prison encouraging the inmates. You'd think you would leave tired, worn out, run-down, and needing to go home and rest after volunteering all day. But just like with Jesus, when you help others, you get fed.

Strength, joy, energy, peace, wisdom, and healing come to those who serve. You should be run-down, but God reenergizes and refreshes you so that at the end of the day you aren't down, you are up. You don't leave low, you leave high. God pays you back.

Every time I leave one of our church services, I feel stronger than when I came in. It doesn't make natural sense. I put out a lot of energy, spend long hours, and shake a lot of hands, but I go home reenergized. Why? Because when you serve others, making their lives better, lifting them, healing those who are hurting, you are blessing them and being blessed yourself. You are being fed. You're being filled back up.

If you're always tired and run-down, with no energy, it may be that you're not doing enough for others. You've got to get your mind off yourself. Go to a retirement home and cheer up someone who is lonely. Bake your neighbor a cake. Coach the Little League team. Call a friend in the hospital.

As you lift others, God will lift you. This should not be something you do every once in a while, when you have extra

Lift others and God will lift you

time. This should be a lifestyle, where it's a part of your nature. You don't have to do something big—just small acts of kindness. A simple word of encouragement can make someone's day.

Victoria was walking through the church hallway after a service one day when she saw a young lady coming toward her in a crowd of people. As she passed her, Victoria looked her in the eyes and said, "You are so beautiful."

They had a five-second conversation, and then they both went on their ways. That young lady told me a couple of weeks later that Victoria's small kindness marked a turning point in her life. She had been through an abusive relationship. She felt so unattractive, so bad about herself, and beaten down by life.

She said when Victoria told her that she was beautiful, it was as if she'd broken the chains holding her back. Something came back to life inside her. The scripture says, "A kind word works wonders." All through the day we can serve God by speaking kind words, offering compliments, giving encouragement, and lifting up those around us.

"You look great today."

"I appreciate you."

"I believe in you."

"I'm praying for your family."

Simple words can make a big difference

You should start doing this at home. It's great to serve people when you're out in public, but don't forget to serve your own family. Husbands should serve their wives.

"Honey, I'm going in the kitchen. Can I bring you anything?"

"Let me run and fill up your car's gas tank so you won't have to do it tomorrow."

"I'll help the kids with their homework. You take a break."

Be a blessing to your spouse.

If we all had this servant's attitude toward our spouses, more marriages could stay together. I know men who expect their wives to do everything for them. "I'm not going to serve her, I expect her to serve me: cook, clean, bring my dinner, make sure my clothes are washed. Keep this house straightened up."

That's not a wife, that's a maid! You can hire somebody to do that. If you want a wife—if you want a friend, a lover, and someone to make your life great—then you have to be willing to serve her.

Bring her breakfast in bed. Pick up your own dirty clothes. Help with the children. Make her feel special. Marriage is not a dictatorship. It's a partnership!

You might say: "Well, Joel, the Bible says the wife should submit to the husband." Yes, but it also says the husband should love his wife like Christ loved the church.

Christ modeled a servant attitude. He had all the power in the world. He was the most influential man who ever lived. Yet He bowed down and washed His disciples' feet. He could have hired someone to do it. He could have asked any of the disciples and they would have done it. He could have called an angel down from heaven and said, "Hey, do me a favor wash their feet. They stink; I don't want to deal with it today. Matthew has some fungus on his toes. John hasn't had a shower in two weeks. Peter needs some Odor Eaters!"

Instead, Jesus pulled out His towel, bowed down, and washed their feet one by one. He gave us His example of service to others so we would know you're never too important to be good to people. You are never too successful. You are never too high to bow down low and serve another person. The more you walk in humility, and the more willing you are to serve others, the higher God can take you.

If you are married, try serving your spouse more, and you'll see your marriage rise to a new level of happiness. I heard about a guy who bragged that he was head of his household and ran everything at home. About that time his wife walked up.

He said: "Yes, I run the vacuum. I run the dishwasher. And I run the lawn mower."

Victoria and I made an agreement when we first married. We said that I would make all the major decisions, and she would make all the minor decisions. It's funny—in twenty-seven years, there's never been a major decision! Victoria says that I am the head of our household, but she's the neck that turns the head.

Look for others to bless

Let me ask you: Who are you serving? Who are you being good to? Who are you lifting up?

Be on the lookout for others you can bless. God puts people in our lives on purpose so we can brighten their days. You should get up every morning and say, "God, show me my assignment today. Help me to be sensitive to the needs of those around me."

I once baptized nearly eight hundred people on one Saturday. Among them was an older man who'd had a stroke. He couldn't walk at all. They rolled him up in a wheel chair. To get in the church baptistery, you have to go up some stairs and then walk down stairs into the water. The younger man pushing him in the wheelchair was about my age. You could tell that he really cared about the man. He went to great lengths to make sure he was okay.

A couple of men helped the older man stand up. Then the younger man put his arms under his legs and his back so he could carry the elderly man into the water, just like you would carry a sleeping baby. It was a very moving scene, watching the younger man go out of his way to help someone so determined to be baptized despite his age and disabilities.

With the young man's help we were able to baptize the elderly man. After we returned him to his wheelchair, I asked the younger man: "Is that your father?"

He shook his head no.

"Is he your uncle, or your relative?" I asked.

The younger man explained that they'd just met in church a few weeks earlier. He said that on the Sunday I announced the baptism date, the older man in the wheelchair turned to him and said, "I wish I could be baptized. I always wanted to, but I had this stroke. I knew I should have done it sooner."

The young man offered to help him achieve his goal to be baptized. The elderly man said he didn't have any family to bring him to church, explaining that he normally took a bus that served people in wheelchairs.

The young man said, "Don't worry, I'll take care of you." He picked up the stranger at his home, helped him get to the baptism at our church, and carried him in and out of the baptistery. They'd only met once before in church.

My prayer is "God help us all to have that same compassion. Help us not to be so busy, so caught up in our own lives that we miss opportunities to serve others." God is asking you, will you carry someone? Maybe not physically, but will you help lighten their loads? Will you help bring their dreams to pass? Will you go out of your way to be good to them?

Be sensitive to the needs of others

Helping less fortunate people is the closest thing to the heart of God. I will never forget the image of that young man carrying the crippled man into the water. I could understand him doing all that for his father, a relative, or a longtime friend, but this was a stranger he'd just met in our church.

He took off his Saturday when he could have been working out, going to the beach, or hanging out with friends. There would have been nothing wrong with just relaxing, but his attitude was "I have an assignment. God has put someone in my path to serve. I can make a difference in his life and brighten his day."

Jesus said, "When you do it to the least of these, you're doing it unto me." I love the fact this young man wasn't looking for credit. He wasn't announcing, "I'm doing a good deed—look at me." He didn't have anyone cheering for him. He was just quietly serving this man.

Nobody would have known they were strangers if I hadn't asked. Remember that when you are good to others and go out of your way to be a blessing—or when you make sacrifices no one knows about—God sees what you are doing. He sees your heart of compassion. Maybe no one else on this earth is singing your praises, but up there all of heaven is cheering you on.

Cheers in heaven

As a leader of Lakewood Church, I receive rewards for my work from those who thank me, clap for me, and cheer me on. I'm very grateful and very flattered. But when no one is clapping for you, when you're not being thanked, or no recognition comes your way, don't become discouraged and think you're being overlooked. Your reward will be greater.

If people give you credit, then you have received a portion of your reward. When nobody gives you credit, then the scripture says, "What you do in secret, God will reward you for in the open." When it comes time for the rewards to be passed out, some of us in the front will have to step back. Then there will be greater rewards handed out to those who worked behind the scenes. There will be accolades to the volunteers who worked year after year without recognition and for those unselfish individuals—like this young man, who sacrificed to help somebody's dream come to pass— who quietly and without fanfare gave their time, money, and energy.

Not long ago one of our ushers went to be with the Lord. He had volunteered at Lakewood Church for nearly thirty years. He was as faithful as can be. I always used to see this older gentleman, who was quiet with a pleasant smile and he always dressed well. I don't know that I ever talked to him personally, but I remember noticing that he was there service after service, year after year. You could count on him to be helping people every week.

My mother officiated at his funeral. One of his requests was that he would be buried wearing his Lakewood usher's badge. So, at his funeral, in his casket, the badge he'd worn for thirty years was pinned to his favorite suit. He was so proud of being an usher. He could have been buried with a lot of other things, but he was so honored to serve others at our church.

When our former usher entered heaven I believe there was a great celebration. I can imagine angels singing, trumpets blowing, people clapping, and an amazing welcoming-home ceremony. There wasn't a lot of applause and fanfare down here for his life of service and kindness, but it did not go unnoticed. It will be rewarded.

The scripture says when Peter went to heaven, Jesus stood up to welcome him. Jesus is normally seated at the right hand of the Father, but I believe there are times—like when our usher arrived, an unsung hero—Jesus says, "You know what? This one deserves a standing ovation."

I heard about an older missionary couple, who spent more than sixty years in Africa helping less fortunate people. They gave their lives to their mission work, and they did so much good.

> *When you serve others, God will stand up to welcome you home*

When they finally retired, the returned home to New York. It just so happened they were booked on the same ship as President Teddy Roosevelt, who was returning from a big hunting expedition. When their ship pulled into the dock, there was all this fanfare. A band was playing. The mayor and other dignitaries were lined up. Flags waved. Confetti rained down from buildings. Balloons floated in the air. It was a huge celebration.

When the president walked off the ship, the crowd went wild. Tens of thousands cheered, waved, and took photos. The landing was reported in newspapers around the world the next day.

The missionary watched all this and said to his wife, "It doesn't seem right that we've given our lives to help others, to serve, to give, and to make a difference, and the president just goes on a big vacation and the whole world welcomes him home. Nobody even knows we exist."

The missionary felt very discouraged as they walked off the boat. Later that night, he prayed, "God I don't understand. The president returns with the fanfare of the world, but we return and nobody even knows we're here."

He heard God's reply come from within his heart: "Son, it's because you're not home yet."

You will be rewarded. There will be a celebration like you've never seen. It won't be with any band you've heard on earth. The angels will be singing, and all of heaven will join in to welcome you home.

If you have been faithful, sacrificed, volunteered, and given to others, be encouraged today. God sees every act of kindness. He sees every good deed. Nothing you've done has gone unnoticed. God saw it, and the good news is you will be rewarded.

Remember, when you do what God asks, you will be fed, refreshed, strengthened, and reenergized. Be on the lookout for ways you can be good to people. If you develop a lifestyle of serving others, God promises you will be great in the kingdom. I believe and declare because you're a giver, you will come in to your reward. You will come in to health, strength, opportunity, promotion, and breakthroughs. You will come into new levels of God's goodness.

CHAPTER EIGHT

Stay Passionate

Studies show that enthusiastic people get better breaks. They're promoted more often, have higher incomes, and live happier lives. That's not a coincidence. The word *enthusiasm* comes from the Greek word *entheos*. *Theos* is a term for "God."

When you're enthusiastic, you are full of God. When you get up in the morning excited about life, recognizing that each day is a gift, you are motivated to pursue your goals. You will have a favor and blessing that will cause you to succeed.

The eighth undeniable quality of a winner is that they stay passionate throughout their lives. Too many people have lost their enthusiasm. At one time they were excited about their futures and passionate about their dreams, but along the way they hit some setbacks. They didn't get the promotions they wanted, maybe a relationship didn't work out, or they had health issues. Something took the wind out of their sails. They're just going through the motions of life; getting up, going to work, and coming home.

God didn't breathe His life into us so we would drag through the day. He didn't create us in His image, crown us with His favor, and equip us with His power so that we would have no enthusiasm.

You may have had some setbacks. The wind may have been taken out of your sails, but this is a new day. God is breathing new life into you. If you shake off the blahs and get your passion back, then

Get your passion back

the winds will start blowing once again—not against you, but for you. When you get in agreement with God, He will cause things to shift in your favor.

On January 15, 2009, Capt. Chesley "Sully" Sullenberger successfully landed a jet airplane in the Hudson River after the plane's engines were disabled by multiple bird strikes. Despite the dangers of a massive passenger plane landing in icy waters, all 155 passengers and crew members survived. It's known as the "Miracle on the Hudson."

Just after the successful emergency landing and rescue, a reporter asked a middle-aged male passenger what he thought about surviving that frightening event. Although he was shaken up, cold and wet, the passenger had a glow on his face, and excitement in his voice when he replied: "I was alive before, but now I'm *really* alive."

After facing a life-and-death situation, the survivor found that his perspective had changed. He recognized each moment as a gift and decided that instead of just living, he would start *really* living.

Seeds of greatness

My question for you is this: Are you *really* alive? Are you passionate about your life or are you stuck in a rut, letting the pressures of life weigh you down, or taking for granted what you have? You weren't created to simply exist, to endure, or to go through the motions; you were created to be *really* alive.

You have seeds of greatness on the inside. There's something more for you to accomplish. The day you quit being excited about your future is the day you quit living. When you quit being passionate about your future, you go from living to merely existing.

In the natural there may not be anything for you to be excited about. When you look into the future, all you see is more of the same. You have to be strong and say, "I refuse to drag through this day with no passion. I am grateful that I'm alive. I'm grateful that I can breathe without pain. I'm grateful that I can hear my children playing. I am grateful that I was not hurt in that accident. I'm grateful that I have opportunity. I'm not just alive—I'm *really* alive."

This is what Paul told Timothy in the Bible: "Stir up the gift, fan the flame." When you stir up the passion, your faith will allow God to do amazing things. If you want to remain passionate, you cannot let what once was a miracle become ordinary. When you started that new job you were so excited. You told all your friends. You knew it was God's favor. Don't lose the excitement just because you've had it for five years.

When you fell in love after meeting the person of your dreams, you were on cloud nine. You knew this match was the result of God's goodness. Don't take it for granted. Remember what God has done.

When your children were born, you cried for joy. Their births were miracles. You were so excited. Now you have teenagers and you're saying, "God, why did you do this to me?"

Don't let what was once a miracle become so common that it's ordinary. Every time you see your children you should say, "Thank you, Lord, for the gift you've given me."

We worked for three years to acquire the former Houston Rockets basketball arena for our church. During that time, it was still for sports and music events. When there wasn't a ball game or concert, Victoria

Stay excited

and I would come up late at night and walk around it. We'd pray and ask God for His favor.

When the city leaders approved our purchase, we celebrated. It was a dream come true. Nearly ten years later, it's easy to get used to. Holding services in such a huge building could become common, ordinary, and routine because we've been doing it so long now. But I have to admit that every time I walk in the building, I can't help but say, "God, thank you. You have done more than I can ask or think."

Live in amazement

We all have seen God's goodness in some way. God opened a door, gave you a promotion, protected you on the freeway, and caused you to meet someone who has been a blessing. It was His hand of favor.

Don't let it become ordinary. We should live in amazement at what God has done. When I look at my children I think, "God, you're amazing." When I see Victoria, I think, "God, you've been good to me." Driving up to my house, I think, "Lord, thank you for your favor."

Don't let your miracles become so common that they don't excite you anymore. I read about this famous surgeon who continued to go to work every day even into his late eighties. He loved medicine. His staff tried to get him to retire and take it easy, but he wouldn't do it. He had invented a certain procedure that he had performed over ten thousand times. It seemed so routine and so ordinary. He'd done it again and again.

The surgeon was asked in an interview if he ever grew tired of performing his procedure and if it ever got old. He said, "No, because I act like every operation is my very first one."

He was saying, "I don't take for granted what God has

allowed me to do. I don't let it become so ordinary that I lose the awe."

What has God done for you? Do you have healthy children? Do you have people to love? Do you have a place to work? Do you realize your gifts and talents come from God? Do you recognize what seemed like a lucky break was God directing your steps?

There are miracles all around us. Don't take them for granted. Don't lose the amazement of God's works. Fan your flames. Stir up your gifts.

Sometimes we hold back, thinking we'll get excited when the next best thing comes along. Only then will we allow that spring back in our step. But I've learned if you aren't happy where you are, you won't get where you want to be.

You need to sow a seed. Maybe nothing exciting is going on; perhaps you're facing big challenges. You could easily grow discouraged and give up on your dreams. But when you go to work with a smile, give it your best, offer kindness to others, you are sowing a seed.

Sow a seed

God will take that seed and grow it to bring something exciting into your life. The scripture tells us God will take us from glory to glory and from victory to victory. You may be in between victories right now, but keep your passion and hold on to your enthusiasm. The good news is another victory is on its way, another level of glory and another level of God's favor.

Put your heart into it

Ecclesiastes says, "Whatever you do, do it with all your heart and you are honoring God." When you give 100 percent effort, you do it to the best of your ability; because you're honoring God, you will have His blessing. That means it will go better. It will be easier and you will accomplish more.

Let's make it practical. When you do the dishes, don't complain; do it with all your heart and you honor God. When you mow the lawn, don't drag around all sour. Mow it with enthusiasm. Mow it like you're on a mission from God.

With every step, thank God that your legs work. Thank God that you're healthy. At the office don't give it a halfhearted effort. Don't just do what is required to get by. You're not working unto people. You're working unto God. Do it with all your heart. Do it with a smile. Give it your very best.

When I was growing up, there was this police officer who directed traffic at the Galleria Mall in Houston. His assignment was to keep people safe on one of the busiest intersections in the city. Traffic could be backed up for five or ten minutes. He didn't just direct traffic like normal, he practically danced while he directed.

Both hands would be constantly moving. He had that whistle and he held his head like a drum major. His feet would dance here and there. He could direct traffic and moonwalk at the same time. He really put on a show.

Drivers pulled over just to watch him. He did not drag through the day. He didn't feel bad about going to work. He was passionate.

That's the way you should be. Don't drag through life. Don't get stuck in a rut. Whatever you do, put your heart into it. Put a spring in your step. Wear a smile on your face. You honor God when you do it with all your heart.

Be the best that you can be

The scripture says God has given us the power to enjoy what's appointed and allotted to us, which means I don't have the power to enjoy your life. You may have more money, more gifts, more friends, and a better job. But if you put me in your life, I will not enjoy it.

You are uniquely created to run your own race. Quit wishing you were someone else or thinking things such as, "If I had his talent…." If God wanted you to have his talent He would give it to you. Take what you have and develop it. Make the most of your gifts.

Instead of thinking things such as, "If I had her looks…," be grateful for the looks God gave you. That's not an accident. The life you have is perfectly matched for you.

Do it with all your heart

Why don't you get excited about your life? Be excited about your looks, your talent, and your personality. When you are passionate about who you are, you bring honor to God. That's when God will breathe in your direction, and the seeds of greatness He's planted on the inside will spring forth.

Really, it's an insult to God to wish you were someone else. You are saying, "God, why did you make me subpar? Why did you make me less than others?"

God didn't make anyone inferior. He didn't create anyone to be second-class. You are a masterpiece. You are fully loaded and totally equipped for the race that's designed for you.

Your attitude should be: "I may not be as tall, as tan, or as talented as someone else, but that's okay. Nobody will ever be a better me. I'm anointed to be me. I'm equipped to me. And not only that, it's also easy to be me."

It's easy to be yourself. It's easy to run your race because you're equipped for what you need. But so many times, people try to be something they are not. I've known dark-skinned people who apply cream to try to be lighter. And I know light-skinned people who go to a tanning bed to try to be darker.

I had an older lady touch my hair at a book signing recently. She said, "Joel, I wish I had that curly hair." Nowadays you can do something about it. If you have straight hair and you want curly hair, you can perm it. If you have gray hair and you want brown hair, dye it. If you have no hair and you want hair, buy it!

Keep working and growing

If you want to stay passionate, you have to stay productive. You have to have a reason to get out of bed in the morning. When you're not producing, you're not growing. You may retire from your job, but don't ever retire from life. Stay busy. Keep using your mind. Keep helping others. Find some way to stay productive. Volunteer at the hospital. Babysit your relatives' children. Mentor a young person.

When you quit being productive, you start slowly dying. God promises if you keep Him in first place, He will give you a long, satisfied life. How long is a long life? Until you are satisfied.

If you quit producing at fifty and you're satisfied, then the promise is fulfilled. I don't know about you, but I've got too much in me to die right now. I'm not satisfied. I have dreams that have yet to be realized. I have messages that I've yet to give. I have children to enjoy, a wife to *raise*...I mean a wife to *enjoy*. I have grandchildren yet to be born.

When I get to be about ninety, and I'm still strong, still healthy, still full of joy, and still good-looking, then I'll say, "Okay God I'm satisfied. I'm ready for my change of address. Let's go."

Some people are too easily satisfied. They quit living at fifty. We don't bury them until they are eighty. Even though they've been alive, they haven't been really living. Maybe they went through disappointments. They had some failures, or somebody did them wrong and they lost their joy. They just settled and stopped enjoying life.

But God has another victory in your future. You wouldn't be breathing if God didn't have something great in front of you. You need to get back your passion. God is not finished with you.

God will complete what he started in your life. The scripture says God will bring us to a flourishing finish—not a fizzling finish. You need to do your part and shake off the self-pity, shake off what didn't work out.

You may have a reason to feel sorry for yourself, but you don't have a right. God said He will take what was meant for your harm and not only bring you out, but also bring you out better off than you were before.

Get in agreement with God

In the Bible, David said, "Lift up your head and the King of glory will come in." As long as your head is down and you are discouraged, with no joy, no passion, and no zeal, the King of glory will not come.

Instead, get up in the morning and say, "Father, thank you for another day. Thank you for another sunrise. I'm excited about this day." When you're really alive, hopeful, grateful, passionate, and productive, then the King of glory, the most high God, will come in. He'll make a way where it looks like there is no way.

We all face difficulties. We have unfair things happen. Don't let it sour your life. I heard the saying, "Trouble is inevitable but misery is optional." Just because you had a bad break doesn't mean your life is over.

I know a popular minister who led his church for many years and was such a great speaker he was in constant demand. But a few years ago, he was diagnosed with Parkinson's disease. He eventually lost the ability to speak. He had to resign from his church. He once was so eloquent, strong, and vibrant, but it looked as if his career was over. It looked as if his best days were behind him.

But just when things started to look really bad for him, he sent me a manuscript with a note: "Joel, as you know, I can't speak anymore, so I've taken up writing. Here's a look at my newest book."

Just because you can't do what you used to do doesn't mean you're supposed to sit on the sidelines. If you can't speak, write. If you can't run, walk. If you can't stand up, just sit up. If you can't dance, shake your head. If you can't sing, tap your foot. Do whatever you can do. As long as you have breath you have something in you. Don't lose your passion.

> *Don't lose your passion*

Think about the apostle Paul: He was thrown in prison at the peak of his career. Just when it was all coming together he had this major disappointment. Paul could have become depressed and thought, "Too bad for me." He could have given up on his dreams. Instead, he kept his passion.

While in prison, he wrote more than half of the New

Testament. What looked like a setback was really a setup for God to do something greater in Paul's life. You may have been through some bad breaks and unfair situations. Stay passionate. God is still on the throne. If you keep your head up, the King of glory will still come in and guide you to where He wants you to be.

Look ahead

It's tempting to go through life looking in the rearview mirror. When you are always looking back, you become focused on what didn't work out, on who hurt you, and on the mistakes you've made, such as:

"If only I would have finished college."

"If only I'd spent more time with my children."

"If only I'd been raised in a better environment."

As long as you're living in regret, focused on the negative things of the past, you won't move ahead to the bright future God has in store. You need to let go of what didn't work out. Let go of your hurts and pains. Let go of your mistakes and failures.

You can't do anything about the past, but you can do something about right now. Whether it happened twenty minutes ago or twenty years ago, let go of the hurts and failures and move forward. If you keep bringing the negative baggage from yesterday into today, your future will be poisoned.

You can't change what's happened to you. You may have

had an unfair past, but you don't have to have an unfair future. You may have had a rough start, but it's not how you start, it's how you finish.

Don't let a hurtful relationship sour your life. Don't let a bad break, a betrayal, a divorce, or a bad childhood cause you to settle for less in life. Move forward and God will pay you back.

Move forward and God will vindicate you. Move forward and you'll come into a new beginning. Nothing that's happened to you is a surprise to God. The loss of a loved one didn't catch God off guard. God's plan for your life did not end just because your business didn't make it, or a relationship failed, or you had a difficult child.

Here's the question: Will you become stuck and bitter, fall into self-pity, blame others, and let the past poison your future? Or will you shake it off and move forward, knowing your best days are still ahead?

The next time you are in your car, notice that there's a big windshield in the front and a very small rearview mirror. The reason the front windshield is so big and the rearview mirror is so small is that what's happened in the past is not nearly as important as what is in your future. Where you're going is a lot more important than where you've been.

Ditch the baggage

If you stay focused on the past, then you'll get stuck where you are. That's the reason some people don't have any joy.

They've lost their enthusiasm. They're dragging around all this baggage from the past.

Someone offended them last week, and they've got that stuffed in their resentment bags. They lost their tempers or said some things they shouldn't have. Now, they've put those mistakes in their bags of guilt and condemnation.

Ten years ago their loved one died and they still don't understand why; their hurt and pain is packed in their disappointment bag. Growing up they weren't treated right— there's another suitcase full of bitterness.

They've got their regret bags, containing all the things they wish they'd done differently. Maybe there is another bag with their divorce in it, and they are still mad at their former spouse, so they've been carrying resentment around for years. If they went to take an airline flight, they couldn't afford it. They've got twenty-seven bags to drag around with them everywhere they go.

Life is too short to live that way. Learn to travel light. Every morning when you get up, forgive those who hurt you. Forgive your spouse for what | *Forgive those who hurt you* | was said. Forgive your boss for being rude. Forgive yourself for mistakes you've made.

At the start of the day, let go of the setbacks and the disappointments from yesterday. Start every morning afresh and anew. God did not create you to carry around all that baggage. You may have been holding on to it for years. It's not going to change until you do something about it. Put your foot down and say, "That's it. I'm not living in regrets. I'm not staying focused on my disappointments. I'm not dwelling on relationships that didn't work out, or on those who hurt me, or how unfairly I was treated. I'm letting go of the past and moving forward with my life."

You should focus on what you can change, not what you cannot change. What's done is done. If somebody offended you, mistreated you, or disappointed you, the hurts can't be undone. You can get bitter—pack it in a bag and carry it around and let it weigh you down—or you can forgive those who hurt you and go on.

If you lost your temper yesterday, you can beat yourself up—put the guilt and condemnation in a bag—or you can ask for forgiveness, receive God's mercy, and do better today.

If you didn't get a promotion you wanted, you can get sour and go around with a chip on your shoulder, or you can shake it off, knowing that God has something better in store.

No matter what happens, big or small, if you make the choice to let it go and move forward, you won't let the past poison your future.

A woman I know went through a divorce years ago. We prayed several times in our services, asking God to bring a good man into her life. One day she met a fine Godly man, who was very successful. She was so happy, but she made the mistake of carrying all her negative baggage from her divorce into the new relationship. She was constantly talking about what she had been through and how she was so mistreated.

She had a victim mentality. The man told me later that she was so focused on her past and so caught up in what she had been through that he just couldn't deal with it. He moved on. That's what happens when we hold on to the hurts and pains of the past. It will poison you wherever you go. You can't drag around all the personal baggage from yesterday and expect to have good relationships. You've got to let it go.

Quit looking at the little rearview mirror and start looking out the great big windshield in front of you. You may have had some bad breaks, but that didn't stop God's plan for your life. He still has amazing things in your future.

When one door closes, stay in faith and God will open another door. If a dream dies, don't sit around in self-pity talking about what you lost, move forward and dream another dream. Your life is not over because you lost a loved one, went through a divorce, lost a job, or didn't get the house you wanted. You would not be alive unless God had another victory in front of you.

Get ready for the new things God has in store

Pastor Dutch Sheets told a story about a forty-year-old lady having open-heart surgery. She had blockage in one of her arteries and had to have bypass surgery. Although this is a delicate procedure, it's considered a routine surgery and performed successfully more than 230,000 times every year.

During the operation, the surgeon clamps off the main vein flowing to the heart and hooks it to a machine that pumps the blood and keeps the lungs working. The heart actually stops beating while the vein is being bypassed.

When the procedure is over and the machine is removed, the warmth from the body's blood normally causes the heart to wake back up and start beating again. If that doesn't work, they have drugs that will wake up the heart.

This lady was on the operating table and the bypass was finished, so they let her blood start flowing, but for some reason her heart did not start beating. They gave her the usual drugs with no success.

She had no heartbeat. The surgeon massaged her heart with his hand to stimulate that muscle and get it beating again, but even that did not work.

The surgeon was so frustrated, so troubled. It looked as if his patient was finished. After doing everything he could medically, he leaned over and whispered in her ear, "Mary, I've done everything I can do. Now I need you to tell your heart to beat again."

He stepped back and heard *bump, bump, bump, bump.* Her heart kicked in and started beating.

Do you need to tell your heart to beat again? Maybe you've been through disappointments and life didn't turn out like you had hoped. Now you're just sitting on the sideline. You've got to get your passion back. Get your fire back. Tell your

God has a new beginning for you

heart to dream again. Tell your heart to love again. Tell your heart to laugh again. Tell your heart to believe again.

Give life all you've got

I have a friend who went through a divorce after twenty-six years of marriage. His wife left him a note saying she had found someone else. He was once an outgoing, fun, and energetic person. But after his wife left him, he was solemn, discouraged, and he had no joy, no life.

I told him what I'm telling you: "This is not the end. God has a new beginning. But you've got to do your part and tell your heart to beat again." Little by little, he recovered his joy, his vision, and his passion.

Then God brought a beautiful lady into his life and they married. He told me a while back that he's happier than he's ever been.

You may have suffered a setback, too, but don't sit around in self-pity. Tell your heart to beat again. Tell your heart to love again. Someone may have done you wrong, but don't let it poison you. Tell your heart to forgive again. Maybe a dream didn't work out, but nothing will change if you just expect more of the same. Tell your heart to dream again.

You may have let the pressures of life weigh you down, and you're all solemn and serious. You need to tell your heart to laugh again. Tell your heart to smile again. Get back your joy. Get back your enthusiasm.

Jesus said in Revelation 2, "I have one thing against you, you have left your first love." The scripture doesn't say you've lost love, the passage says you've left your first love. That means you can go get it. You haven't lost your passion. You just left it. Go get it.

You haven't lost the love for your family; you've just left it—now go get it. You haven't lost that dream; it's still there in you. You just left it. You have to go get it.

Stir up what God put on the inside. Fan the flame. Don't be just barely alive. God wants you to be really alive.

You may have had some setbacks, but this is a new day. Dreams are coming back to life. Your vision is being renewed. Your passion is being restored. Hearts are beating again. Get ready for God's goodness. Get ready for God's favor.

You *can* live a life of victory. You *can* overcome every obstacle. You *can* accomplish your dreams. You *can* set new levels for your family.

Not only are you able, but I also declare you *will* become all God created you to be. You *will* rise to new levels. You *will* live a blessed, successful, rewarding life. My encouragement is: Don't settle where you are.

You have seeds of greatness on the inside. Put these principles into action each day. Get up in the morning expecting good things, go through the day positive, focused on your vision, running your race, knowing that you are well able.

Winning is in your DNA. The most high God breathed

His life into you. You've got what it takes. This is your time. This is your moment. Shake off doubts, shake off fear and insecurity, and get ready for favor, get ready for increase, get ready for the fullness of your destiny. You can, you will!

We Want to Hear from You!

Each week, I close our international television broadcast by giving the audience an opportunity to make Jesus the Lord of their lives. I'd like to extend that same opportunity to you.

Are you at peace with God? A void exists in every person's heart that only God can fill. I'm not talking about joining a church or finding religion. I'm talking about finding life and peace and happiness. Would you pray with me today? Just say, "Lord Jesus, I repent of my sins. I ask You to come into my heart. I make You my Lord and Savior."

Friend, if you prayed that simple prayer, I believe you have been "born again." I encourage you to attend a good, Bible-based church and keep God in first place in your life. For free information on how you can grow stronger in your spiritual life, please feel free to contact us.

Victoria and I love you, and we'll be praying for you. We're believing for God's best for you, that you will see your dreams come to pass. We'd love to hear from you!

To contact us, write to:

Joel and Victoria Osteen
P.O. Box 4600
Houston, TX 77210

Or you can reach us online at www.joelosteen.com.

STAY**CONNECTED,**
BE**BLESSED.**

From thoughtful articles to powerful blogs, podcasts and more, JoelOsteen.com is full of inspirations that will give you encouragement and confidence in your daily life.

AVAILABLE ON JOELOSTEEN.COM

 today'sW◯RD

This daily devotional from Joel and Victoria will help you grow in your relationship with the Lord and equip you to be everything God intends you to be.

Joel Osteen
STREAMING

Miss a broadcast? Watch Joel Osteen on demand, and see Joel LIVE on Sundays.

Joel Osteen
PODCAST

The podcast is a great way to listen to Joel where you want, when you want.

CONNECT WITH US

Join our community of believers on your favorite social network.

PUT JOEL IN YOUR POCKET

Get the inspiration and encouragement of Joel Osteen on your iPhone, iPad or Android device! Our app puts Joel's messages, devotions and more at your fingertips.

Thanks for helping us make a difference in the lives of millions around the world.